DEVOTED TO LIFE

A 365 DAY DEVOTIONAL
TO RESTORE AMERICA'S GREATNESS

By

Leslie H. Young, D.B.S., Ph.D.

Author of "4 X 4 Love – For Life's Off-road Experiences"

DEVOTED TO LIFE

Copyright 2019 by Leslie H. Young
Encouragement for End-times Endurance
www.encouragementforendtimesendurance.com
Telford, TN 37690
ISBN 9780578443072

Printed in the United States of America

We are honored that you dedicated this devotional to our beloved son. May the Lord be glorified through this body of work and may the saints come to the realization that the gates of hell cannot prevail against the obedient church of the living God!

IN KING JESUS' SERVICE,
Rev. Rusty Lee Thomas
National Director, Operation Save America
Author: "Raising Godly Children in a Godless Age"

Les Young is man who has a heart that pants after God and His precious preborn children. He is a brother who has allowed the theology of heaven to become biography in the streets of his city. The Word of God has become flesh through him. Isn't this what the miracle of Christmas is all about? Each day of the year we are encouraged in this devotional to "...keep our eye on the prize" and speak for those who cannot speak for themselves.

Rev. Philip "Flip" Benham
Former National Director Operation Save America
Baptized Norma McCorvey (The "Jane Roe" in the Roe v. Wade decision)

Our Dad, Flip Benham, has said for years, "Abortion will end when the church says so and not a minute sooner." Francis Schaeffer used to say, "In front of every abortion clinic in America there should be a sign that reads, 'Open by permission of the church.'" Les Young has written a devotional that points the church towards her duty to defend the pre-born, providing a roadmap of activities that are non-threatening weapons which every Christian can use to pull down the stronghold of abortion.

David & Jason Benham
The Benham Brothers
Best Selling Authors of "Whatever the Cost" and Living Among Lions"
Founders and CEO's of The Benham Companies

Dr. Les Young's Pro-Life Devotional is an inspirational literary work which inspires and reminds us of the challenge that we face with eradicating abortion. Halting the shedding of innocent blood in this nation may seem like an impossible task, but we need to remind ourselves that with God all things are possible, and this wonderful devotional encourages us to believe for just that.

Daniel Secomb
Founding Director of Israel, Islam, and the End Times
Author: "The Politics of the Last Days"

Dr. Les Young has been a true advocate of and spokesman for the sanctity of life for many years. His ministry for the unborn and their parents has been a blessed example, helping many in the body of Christ know how to pray and how to stand for life. I thank the Lord for his writings and for this "Devoted to Life" book, which will encourage its readers to choose life, and to help others do the same.

Linda Edwards
Area Coordinator
40 Days for Life, Tri-Cities, Tennessee

As a leader of Operation Save America - CT for 28 years I strongly endorse Pastor Les Young's book DEVOTED TO LIFE. He has been involved in this ministry for many years and has a heart to end the terrible sin of abortion in America and the world. I believe reading this book will draw your heart closer to God's heart and help you hate abortion like He does. We need to help open the eyes of those around us so that they would see abortion as an abomination to God our Creator.

For the Least of These,
Marilyn Carroll
Director, OSA-CT

In no other time of human history have so many unborn children been killed through the act of abortion. Millions are sacrificed each year on the altar of choice and convenience. We desperately need voices calling a generation to repent, remember, and resolve that life is precious and God-given. Dr. Les Young is one of those voices. Dr. Young has been standing for life for decades and calling the church and the culture to protect humanity. In, Devoted to Life, Dr. Young encourages us to daily call on the Giver of Life as we contend for those "appointed to die."-Proverbs 31:8 (NKJV)

Jeffrey Oakes
Senior Pastor
Hosanna Fellowship
Johnson City, TN

Pro-life conversations have been limited to election cycles and political debates, but the pro-life truth is not merely a political issue or a rightful fight against abortion. The theological principles that form the pro-life reality need to permeate much more of our culture and our own personal worldviews. How much stronger would our fight against the killing of the unborn become when the counter principles become ingrained in our being. And how much more Biblical and God-glorifying would our lives become if we meditated on the Scriptural case for life. In my time in ministry, I have found there is no better life-changing study method or resource than a thematic daily devotional. I'm thankful that Dr. Les Young has created this unique and transformative tool."

Jake McCandless – Pastor, Author, and Executive Director of Stand Firm Ministries

ACKNOWLEDGMENTS

I wish to express sincere appreciation for Operation Save America (OSA) and Operation Save America – Connecticut (OSA-CT) for first drawing me into the battle for the sanctity of life from the moment of conception. The consistent dedication of people like Flip Benham, Rusty Thomas, and Marilyn Carroll have been an inspiration to continue the fight. Others like Cal Zastrow and Linda Edwards have continued to fan the flame. And my wife Barbara, as always, has encouraged me in every step, providing editorial guidance along the way. My prayer is that this book will raise the awareness level of the church concerning what has become the National Sin of the United States of America. May thousands more be encouraged and empowered to pray, witness and counsel at the abortion mills, and to contact their congressmen on a regular basis demanding passage of Personhood/Life at Conception Legislation.

And let us not grow weary of doing good, for in due season we will reap, if we do not give up. **Galatians 6:9 (ESV)**

DEDICATION

This book is dedicated to Jeremiah Thomas.

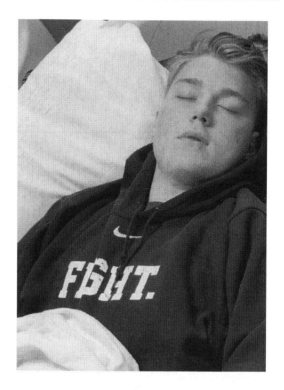

Jeremiah's Letter to His Generation: A Call Back to Christ and Abolish Abortion

There are many ways to be brave in this world.

Sometimes bravery involves laying down your life for something bigger than yourself or for someone else.

Sometimes bravery involves giving up everything you have ever known, or everyone you have ever loved, or everything you've ever wanted, for the sake of something greater.

But sometimes it doesn't.

Sometimes bravery is nothing more than gritting your teeth through pain. It is bearing down through the hard work of every day life. The slow walk towards a better life.

And sometimes it's letting go.

Hey guys, my name is Jeremiah Thomas. I was raised on the front lines of the ongoing battle for the soul of our nation called abortion. It is a hidden holocaust that has wiped out one third of our generation. I'm from a family of 12 siblings, a stay-at-home mom, and a fiery preacher for a dad. I remember growing up watching my father fearlessly preach and plead with women going into death camps. As a result, I always wanted to grow up to be a preacher.

One thing you should know about my family. We are really big on sports. Both the boys and girls. The football and volleyball seasons are huge for us. I am the youngest of the guys in the family. So naturally growing up meant I got destroyed playing backyard football.

I learned a lot from my older brothers. I watched them all practice. I watched them all play. I watched them all win State. I wanted to be THAT good.

My brothers played for a private Christian school that allowed homeschoolers to participate. For two years, I woke up early and drove with them to practice so I could be the team's water boy. The school's athletic policy changed right before I got my chance to play. Only enrolled students were allowed on the team. So, in the fifth grade, my parents enrolled me because they had promised me the opportunity to play football and my Dad never goes back on his word.

After some years of flag football practice, my turn to play tackle football finally came in the seventh grade. We went 9-1 ending my junior high career on a good note. My parents pulled me out immediately after my last game and brought me back to homeschooling. I skipped 8th grade and went straight into my freshman year. I played with a different Christian school, the Parkview Pacers. I played with them my freshman and sophomore year, winning state my sophomore year. This meant that all the Thomas' boys had won State. I received awards and got selected both years to play in the "All Star Game." I don't say this to brag but to share what my life was before cancer.

Growing up, I always had one foot in Christ and one foot in the world. I attended church, did Bible study, and ministered with my family but when I was at school or hanging with friends you couldn't tell that I knew Christ.

It wasn't until the summer of 2017 in Louisville, Kentucky that I experienced revival. I was baptized along with forty-eight other kids (and some adults). I came home to Waco, Texas on fire for Christ.

I immediately ran to the roar of the battle and began to do ministry outside our local abortion clinic. With my Bible and a handheld microphone, I began sharing the Gospel on high school and college campuses.

Football came and went way too fast. It was a great season. We won State! Football season became basketball season. I continued to minister and play sports.

One night before Christmas, our family watched the Muppet Christmas Carol. I cried through the whole film. I thought I was feeling the Christmas spirit, but I soon realized it was the presence of God.

I was so moved, after the movie, I offered to do all the dishes for my siblings. My dad told me, it was our "Christmas miracle."

There were a lot of dishes and it was late. My tired sisters mumbled a "thank you" as they went off to their bedrooms. My parents and older brother went to bed too, leaving me alone to do dishes.

As I started washing the dishes, I regretted my decision. I decided to worship the Lord. I started to cry again, which then turned to weeping. Soon it was too much for me. I couldn't do the dishes. I tried to run to my bedroom, so I could collapse on my bed. But I didn't make it; I collapsed in my dad's office.

For the next two hours I was pinned to the ground, shaking in the presence of God. At that point, deep intercession and travail filled me, leaving me undone. I knew God was demanding more of me. I began to hear a Voice. It was almost like it was speaking into me. I recognized the words the Voice was saying, when I knew that I shouldn't. It spoke in a different language, saying the names of the Lord. It was the Lord! He was speaking to me! I woke up to see my brother, Valiant, and my dad sitting in chairs around me.

"What just happened?" I heard my Dad say.

After I recovered, Valiant and my other brother, Josiah, had about an hour-long worship session in our bedroom. The presence of the Lord was in the room. It was so thick, you could cut with a knife. But this time His presence was sweet and convicting, causing my brothers and me to weep and hug each other as we confessed our sins to one other.

Fast forward, basketball season was almost over. After a game, I came home with a small injury. A little bump on my ribs. Thinking it was your average rib injury, I wrapped it up and finished the basketball season. It was hurting a lot more by baseball season, but I had already started playing, so I kept my commitment.

I kept my ribs well wrapped and it didn't give me too much of a problem. It wasn't until I got home and tried to fall asleep that I would have major problems. I couldn't sleep to save my life. My ribs hurt, and my back hurt as well. The back pain was excruciating. Sometimes I would pound the ground with my fist and cry out. My mom or dad would wake up and hold me as I grimaced in pain.

The first doctor said the pain was scoliosis in my back and a contusion on my ribs. But the pain only grew worse. We went back to the doctor's office and they took a CT scan. The doctor said we would have to wait for the radiologist to read the scan. We went home expecting to come back sometime next week. As soon as we entered our house, the doctor's office called us saying we needed to get back A.S.A.P.

My parents and I headed back with a bit of anxiety. The doctor received us back into his office and sat us down. The next few moments were a blur as my world was turned upside down and inside out. The only thing I could really understand was that I had a tumor in my front chest and it was malignant. I was dying.

My dream to play college football was DEAD. My dream to minister was DEAD. We were absolutely blindsided. I was the healthiest I had ever been. I was in my prime! I had so many plans and goals for the year. I couldn't accept the news that I had a malignant tumor, not yet. Not now. Maybe a tumor at seventy years old; I could die at seventy. Not at sixteen.

I was in full-time ministry mode at that time. I went out to my local abortion mill, Baylor college, and high schools. I would share the Gospel of the Kingdom with complete strangers to fulfill the Great Commission. I was pursuing the call that was on my life. I thought I could only serve God if I was healthy. I thought if I was hospitalized, I would lose all opportunity to minister to others. Little did I know that God was going to use my sickness to reach the lost and encourage brethren throughout the world.

After a few months of cancer and a bunch of different treatments, here I am. I'm lying down in bed, typing this letter. I have lost my hair, my ability to walk, fifty pounds of healthy muscle, the sensation in my legs and back, and my football career. But I haven't lost my faith and hope in God. In fact, my faith in Him has been strengthened. I have grown so much closer to my Savior, knowing full well my life is in His hands. He has been with me every step of the way, guiding me and teaching me.

I've learned no matter what you get hit with in life, you sometimes have to lower your shoulder and keep trucking, just like in football. Trust God to keep your feet and sustain you. In less time than it takes to play a full football season, my life has been taken over by cancer. I don't know how much time I have left on this earth, but with what time I do have, I want it to count for God and my generation. This is my call to my generation, "Leave it all behind and come back home!"

"This day I call the heavens and the earth as witnesses against you that I have set before you life and death, blessings and curses. Now choose life, so that you and your children may live" (Deuteronomy 30:19).

We have grown up in a culture of death, sexual confusion, immorality and fatherlessness. This culture of death I speak of consists of abortion, homosexuality and suicide. One third of our generation has been wiped out due to abortion. Over 25 million people have died as a result of AIDS. Even without AIDS, the life expectancy of a homosexual man or woman is about 33 years shorter than that of a heterosexual. More young people die from suicide than from cancer, heart disease, AIDS, birth defects, stroke, pneumonia, influenza, and chronic lung disease, combined.

We have been handed a bill of goods that has completely destroyed us. In our nation, we have chosen death and received the curse.

I would like to use a parable of the Prodigal Son to describe our generation. We have taken our Heavenly Father's blessings and have turned from Him. We've squandered our godly heritage and we still haven't turned back to the Father. How bad does it have to get in order for our generation to wake up and realize that we are a long way from home?

My call to you today is to come back to the Father. Leave behind the darkness, deception and despair. We are a fatherless and lawless generation searching for identity. Meanwhile, our heavenly Father is standing with arms wide open, beckoning to us to return to Him through the good news of the Gospel of the Kingdom of our Lord and Savior, Jesus Christ.

If you're going through depression, there's hope in Christ. If you're battling disease, there's healing in Christ. If you're contemplating suicide or abortion, there's abundant life in Christ.

Abortion is more than wrong. It's an abomination. It's the murder of an innocent baby. It turns mothers into murderers and men into cowards. Abortion goes against everything God intended. He made men to protect women and children. He made women to love and nurture. So, in conclusion, abortion is more than just a "woman's issue." It's an act of murder that should be penalized by law. It is our generation's duty to rise up and abolish abortion.

It's time to wake up and stand against the evil in our day. There's a battle to fight and souls to save. Everybody else is joining in the confusion and chaos that is ruining our nation. They are literally killing themselves and others trying to prove that they are right. True rebellion is going against the flow of what everybody else is doing.

Finally, to the liberal student activists who think they are fighting "the establishment" on college campuses- you are the establishment! Your professors are liberal. Your parents are probably liberal. Your friends are liberal. The music you listen to is liberal. Hollywood is liberal so the movies you watch are liberal.

Who or what are you truly rebelling against?

To the college kids who complain that they can't trust our government- you're doing everything in your power to make it bigger. The government is taking away our natural, God given rights. You're making the problem worse. This is insanity.

If you want to be a rebel on college campuses fight for freedom! Stir the status quo, don't go along with it. True examples of counter culture are the Christians who fight against abortion. They're actually fighting to end the grave evil in our day.

Look at history. Over one hundred million people have been murdered under the ideologies of Democratic Socialism and Communism. When we forget our history, history will always repeat itself. That's why one third of our generation has been wiped out by abortion. That's why our rights are slowly being ripped out of our Constitution. That's why the establishment is evil.

It's time for my generation to wake up. It is time leave our sin, unbelief, rebellion, and lust behind. Let's make a journey of saving faith back to the Father's House. It is there and there only that we will find light, love, and life through Jesus Christ our Lord!

It is my sincere prayer that you who read this will take my words to heart, change your mind, and be reconciled to the Lord through the merits of Jesus Christ. May God's Kingdom come and His will be done on earth as it is in heaven in Jesus' name!

Penned and published by Jeremiah Thomas 6/24/2018

Jeremiah's body succumbed to cancer and his spirit went to be with Jesus on 8/26/2018.

INTRODUCTION

This book had a secret beginning. At the start of the Fall 2017 40 Days for Life campaign I began a daily pro-life post on Facebook. Initially the posts were slightly modified copies of what appeared in the 40 Days for Life emails. As the campaign neared its close, the Lord impressed me with the fact that the abortion holocaust would continue. It wasn't long before I was prompted to continue the daily posts.

There soon appeared on my timeline a post titled "Day 41 of 365 Days for Life." I was now committed, and my commitment had been made public. For the next 318 days I made a pro-life post, with the day number changing along with the Scripture and prayer focus. On day 359 I asked the Lord what I should do when day 365 arrived and beyond. He said, "Write a pro-life devotional."

My initial reaction was like that of Sarai in Genesis 18:12. I laughed to myself and began to remind the Lord that devotional writing was not my genre of choice. I argued that I couldn't do this. It was then that He reminded me that I had already done it, one day at a time. Thus this devotional is a collection of heartfelt messages, written one day at a time, with no end game in mind. God's ways are amazing.

Over the years I have become a bit of a history buff. It doesn't take much for me to become engrossed in biographical stories about the founding fathers of the United States of America. I have come to know them as flawed men, just like the rest of us; yet they were driven to form a new nation based on the biblical principles of life, liberty, and the pursuit of happiness. "Make America Great Again" has become a mantra in recent years, popular with some, hated by others. It is my opinion that we cannot be great (again or ever) unless we return to those founding principles – the first of which is LIFE! Righteousness exalts a nation, but sin is a reproach to any people." (Proverbs 14:34 ESV)

As God directed me do something more to advance the cause of life, so He has something more for you to do. Please go to the Epilogue for some suggestions. God bless you.

January 1

*"I call heaven and earth to witness against you
today, that I have set before you life and death,
blessing and curse. Therefore choose life, that you
and your offspring may live,"*
(Deuteronomy 30:19)

Father God, today we pray that multitudes would
"Choose Life" because the Lord of life, Jesus
Christ, said so! One of His stated purposes for
coming was that we might have life in abundance.
Too many are denied that opportunity by the hand
of man. May that end soon, both by choice and by
law. In Jesus' Name, Amen!

January 2

"He has told you, O man, what is good; and what does the Lord require of you but to do justice, and to love kindness, and to walk humbly with your God?"
(Micah 6:8)

Lord God. we pray because "the effectual fervent prayers" of righteous people are powerful, and mixed with our presence at the abortion centers, it is exponentially powerful. Help us to each find our place in the fight for life may Your Spirit keep us diligent and persistent until legalized abortion is no more. In Jesus' Name, Amen!

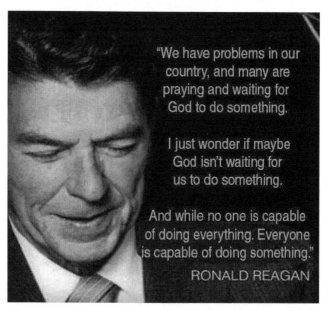

"We have problems in our country, and many are praying and waiting for God to do something.

I just wonder if maybe God isn't waiting for us to do something.

And while no one is capable of doing everything. Everyone is capable of doing something."
RONALD REAGAN

January 3

"Because the sentence against an evil deed is not executed speedily, the heart of the children of man is fully set to do evil."
(Ecclesiastes 8:11)

Loving heavenly Father, help us to see the worth of all human beings by the way in which you care for each of us. Provide us with the faith, grace and courage to protect that which is so precious to you. And may we do this without apology or excuse. In Jesus' Name, Amen!

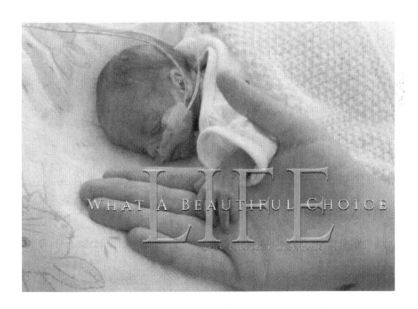

January 4

"The great city was split into three parts, and the cities of the nations fell, and God remembered Babylon the great, to make her drain the cup of the wine of the fury of his wrath."
(Revelation 16:19)

Lord God Almighty, You know all too well that abortion is the leading cause of death in the world ... with an estimated 56 million happening every year. As a result, some of the campaigns have taken on an international flavor. Thank you for the pro-life efforts that are active all over the world. While we have no idea how much more of this genocide can happen before the cup of Your wrath is full, may we remain faithful until righteousness is restored. In Jesus' Name, Amen!

January 5

The King will answer and say to them, "Assuredly,
I say to you, inasmuch as you did it to one of the
least of these my brethren, you did it to me."
(Matthew 25:41)

Gracious and merciful Father, we renew our
dedication to defending the unborn and all whose
right to life is compromised by our godless
society's selfish lack of concern. Free us from our
own failures and sins so that we will be truly pro-
life in every area of our lives. In Jesus' Name,
Amen!

January 6

The Spirit of the Lord is upon Me, because He has anointed Me to preach the gospel to the poor; He has sent Me to heal the brokenhearted, to proclaim liberty to the captives and recovery of sight to the blind, to set at liberty those who are oppressed.
(Luke 4:18)

Lord, send us to the poorest, the most broken, the most captive, the most blind and the most oppressed in the world - the innocent pre-born children in their mother's wombs that are scheduled for destruction. Help us to bring them healing, liberty, sight and justice through Jesus Christ our Lord, Amen.

January 7

Jesus said: "A man was going down from Jerusalem to Jericho, when he fell into the hands of robbers. They stripped him of his clothes, beat him and went away, leaving him half dead. A priest ... passed by on the other side. So, too, a Levite... passed by on the other side. But a Samaritan... came where the man was; and when he saw him, he took pity on him."
(Luke 10:30-33)

Father, we are moved by the lesson of the Good Samaritan, who allowed compassion to influence him more than fear. Give us the same heart. Grant that we may never count the cost of standing up and speaking out for the unborn as something we are unwilling to pay. In Jesus' Name, Amen!

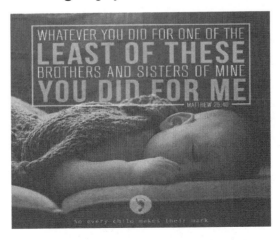

January 8

"Your eye shall not pity him, but you shall purge the guilt of innocent blood from Israel, so that it may be well with you."
(Deuteronomy 19:13)

Father, at one abortuary the address aptly describes what goes on here with the permission of the state (by law) and of the church (by silence). Please move the church to speak so powerfully and effectively that the laws are changed, all for Your glory, In Jesus' Name, Amen!

January 9

"Rescue the weak and the needy; deliver them from the hand of the wicked."
(Psalm 82:4)

Father, may you empower the hundreds today who are serving in our pregnancy help centers. Grant those answering calls, providing ultrasound and following up with a bold spirit of truth, love and perseverance. May their work to preserve life not be in vain. In Jesus' Name, Amen!

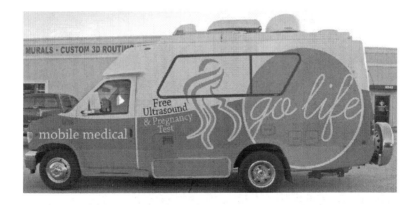

January 10

"I beseech you to walk worthy of the calling with which you were called, with all lowliness, and gentleness, with longsuffering, bearing with one another in love."
(Ephesians 4:1b-2)

Dear Heavenly Father, we are humbled that you have called us and appointed us to be ambassadors of Christ in a world that is not our home. We pray that your Holy Spirit will empower us to walk worthy of the calling. We pray that Your unconditional love will flow through us to those who desperately need Your saving grace, especially those struggling with choices of life and death. May they find the grace to choose life. In Jesus' Name, Amen!

January 11

"My power is made perfect in weakness."
(2 Corinthians 12:9)

Lord, during events like Forty Days for Life, we ask that each day everything in us separating us from your perfect will would be pruned from our hearts and souls. May we submit our weakness to you when it comes to the fight for life. In the blessed freedom of your strength may we experience a powerful anointing of your Holy Spirit that produces victory. In Jesus' Name, Amen!

January 12

"A father of the fatherless, a defender of widows, is God in His holy habitation."
(Psalm 68:5)

Heavenly Father, we thank you for caring about each of us so deeply. Help us to see and know you as our Father in heaven each and every day of our lives. As we speak out today in behalf of life, may your loving hand rest on every child carried in its mother's womb. May they be born into this world and come to know fully and personally your endless love.

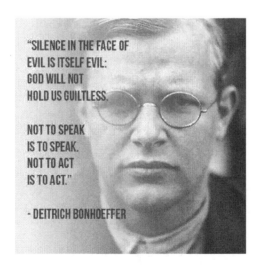

"SILENCE IN THE FACE OF EVIL IS ITSELF EVIL: GOD WILL NOT HOLD US GUILTLESS.

NOT TO SPEAK IS TO SPEAK. NOT TO ACT IS TO ACT."

- DEITRICH BONHOEFFER

January 13

"Let all bitterness, and wrath, and anger, and clamor, and evil speaking, be put away from you, with all malice. And be kind one to another, tenderhearted, forgiving one another, even as God for Christ's sake has forgiven you."
Ephesians 4:31-32

Dearest God, You tell us in Proverbs that the foolish and the wicked lack wisdom and understanding. I pray you will trouble the souls of those in the abortion industry so that they hunger for truth and cry out for freedom. May the goodness of God overcome the evil of abortion. In Jesus' Name, Amen!

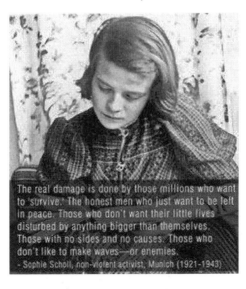

The real damage is done by those millions who want to 'survive.' The honest men who just want to be left in peace. Those who don't want their little lives disturbed by anything bigger than themselves. Those with no sides and no causes. Those who don't like to make waves—or enemies.
- Sophie Scholl, non-violent activist, Munich (1921-1943)

January 14

"Now Cain talked with Abel his brother; and it came to pass, when they were in the field, that Cain rose up against Abel his brother and killed him. Then the Lord said to Cain, 'Where is Abel your brother?' He said, 'I do not know. Am I my brother's keeper?'"
(Genesis 4:8-9)

Father, help us to embrace the fact that we are our "brother's keeper" and our brethren include babies in the womb. When, due to selfish motives, we try to cast off this responsibility please call to us to account. May our words and actions with respect to these, the least of Christ's brethren, be pleasing to You. In Jesus' Name, Amen!

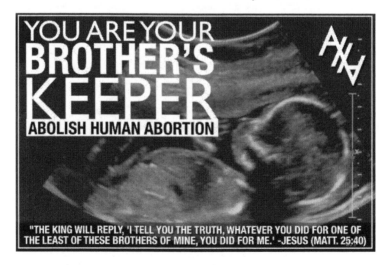

January 15

"How could one chase a thousand, And two put ten thousand to flight, Unless their Rock had sold them, And the LORD had surrendered them?"
(Deuteronomy 32:30 NKJV)

Father God, Harry S. Truman parroting the above Scripture said, "It is amazing what you can accomplish if you do not care who gets the credit." We want all the credit, all the glory and all the thanks to go to our Lord and Savior, Jesus Christ for all He has done through various organizations laboring for the end of abortion. End it now; in His Name we pray, Amen!

January 16

"And the Lord God formed man of the dust of the ground, and breathed into his nostrils the breath of life; and man became a living being."
(Genesis 2:7)

Lord, we are yours. Thank you for breathing into us the breath of life. Thank you for claiming us as your own. May our words and actions in defense of human life proclaim to all the world that you alone are Lord of life and death; Lord of our freedom and of our choices. May we value the inalienable right of life for all, beginning from the moment of conception. In Jesus' Name, Amen!

"We hold these truths to be self-evident, that all men are created equal, that they are endowed by their Creator with certain unalienable Rights, that among these are Life..."

January 17

"Behold, children are a heritage from the Lord, the fruit of the womb is a reward. Like arrows in the hand of a warrior, so are the children of one's youth. Happy is the man who has his quiver full of them; they shall not be ashamed, but shall speak with their enemies in the gate."
(Psalm 127:3-5)

Heavenly Father, please keep us from taking for granted the gift of children. Help us to remember this heritage that you have given us. Make us faithful stewards of these precious lives; that each generation might be raised in the nurture and admonition of the Lord. Help us to remember that a baby is the offspring of both a mother and a father. Help us to navigate the difficult path of protecting the biblical rights of each. In Jesus' Name, Amen!

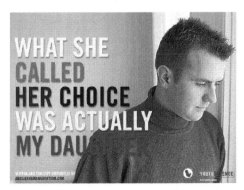

January 18

"If I have despised the cause of my male or female servant when they complained against me, what then shall I do when God rises up? When He punishes, how shall I answer Him? Did not He who made me in the womb make them? Did not the same One fashion us in the womb?"
(Job 31:13-15)

God, forgive us when we try to explain away the obligation we have to help others who need help. Enable us to not devalue them because of the circumstance that they are in, but to see them for what they are; people who, like us, were formed by your hand in their mother's womb. May those caught up in the culture of death receive a divine break-through, so they can see the truth. In Jesus' Name, Amen!

January 19

"Isaac prayed to the Lord for his wife because she was barren; and the Lord granted his prayer and Rebekah his wife conceived. The children struggled together within her… So she went to inquire of the Lord. And the Lord said to her, 'Two nations are in your womb, and two peoples, born of you, shall be divided; the one shall be stronger than the other, the elder shall serve the younger.'"
(Genesis 25:21-23)

O, God, you formed us in our mother's womb and planned a unique and special life and purpose for each of us, and we do thank you. Grant that we may pray and work for an end to abortion, so that no unborn baby you have made may fail to achieve your divine intention for him or her because of intentional murdera. In Jesus' Name, Amen!

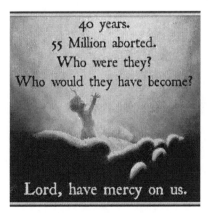

6 Years later the number has grown to 61 million plus!

January 20

"For we do not wrestle against flesh and blood, but against principalities, against powers, against the rulers of the darkness of this age, against spiritual hosts of wickedness in the heavenly places. Therefore, take up the whole armor of God, that you may be able to withstand in the evil day and having done all, to stand."
-- Ephesians 6:12-13

Dear Lord, as you lead us in the spiritual battle against abortion may we be reminded that the battle is truly Yours. Help us to be silent no more. Thank you for hearing our requests for direction and protection. Thank you for the victory that is ours because of Your Son Jesus, in whose Name we pray, Amen!

If a minute of silence was observed for every baby aborted since *Roe v. Wade*, we would be silent for over 100 years.

www.hli.org

January 21

"But God chose what is foolish in the world to shame the wise; God chose what is weak in the world to shame the strong;"
(1 Corinthians 1:27)

Lord, individually we seem weak, but if 10% of the 80 million evangelical Christians in this nation would call their 3 congressmen once a month demanding passage of personhood legislation it would require 5 staffers in each office working full time just to receive these calls. It would be unprecedented. It would change things. So we bow before you today and honestly confess that You have every right to turn a deaf ear to our prayers if we are unwilling to take 3-4 minutes a month to "put feet to our prayers." Convict us and move us to be silent no more, in Jesus' Name, Amen!

January 22

"Woe to him who builds his house by unrighteousness And his chambers by injustice…"
(Jeremiah 22:13a NKJV)

Almighty God, on this date in 1973, seven black-robed judges determined that the so-called "Personhood Amendment" (14th) applied more to privacy than it did to human life in the womb. They circumvented both constitutional law and natural law, setting the stage for legalized infanticide in the land. May the Judge of all the earth come and enact true justice and restore righteousness to the land. In Jesus' Name, Amen!

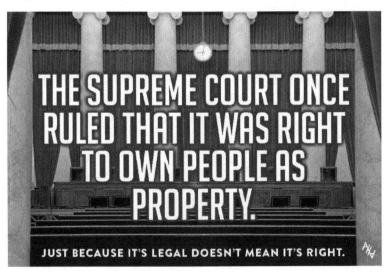

THE SUPREME COURT ONCE RULED THAT IT WAS RIGHT TO OWN PEOPLE AS PROPERTY.

JUST BECAUSE IT'S LEGAL DOESN'T MEAN IT'S RIGHT.

January 23

"Now these are Your servants and Your people, whom You have redeemed by Your great power, and by Your strong hand. O Lord, I pray, please let Your ear be attentive to the prayer of Your servant, and to the prayer of Your servants who desire to fear Your name."
(Nehemiah 1:10-11)

Lord God, we pray for your continued guidance and protection of all those engaged in the fight for life, as long as the battle rages. May we be steadfast, unmovable, always abounding in Your work, knowing that our labor will not be in vain. May legalized abortion on demand end and may Personhood from the moment of conception be the law of the land. In Jesus' Name, Amen!

January 24

*"Then the word of the Lord came to me, saying:
'Before I formed you in the womb I knew you;
Before you were born I sanctified you; I ordained
you a prophet to the nations.'"*
(Jeremiah 1:4-5)

Lord God, we confess that in You we live and
move and have our being. Because You are, we
are. May we find grace from You to affirm the
value of every human being, from the moment of
conception until natural death, and may we labor
to make this truth known to the world around us.
Our desire is to see life celebrated in our culture, to
Your great glory. In Jesus' Name, Amen!

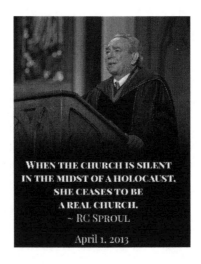

January 25

"These all wait for you, that you may give them their food in due season, what you give them they gather in; you open your hand they are filled with good. You hide your face, they are troubled; you take away their breath, they die and return to their dust. You send forth your Spirit, they are created; and you renew the face of the earth."
(Psalm 104:27-30)

Beloved Father, remind us today that there is no truth but you, and Truth says, "...therefore, choose life!" Remind us that You, who created all life, are in control of all life. It is for You to choose the moment when physical life begins and ends. May we always choose life; may our laws reflect the choice of life, and may we trust you with every aspect of life. In Jesus' Name, Amen!

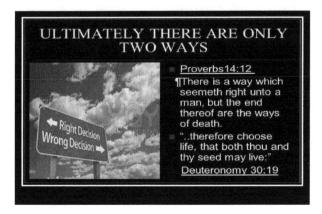

January 26

"For judgment is without mercy to one who has shown no mercy. Mercy triumphs over judgment."
(James 2:13)

You O God are a good and merciful God. The murder of innocent babies in the womb is deserving of nothing but judgment, but for all who will forsake their wicked ways and turn to You, You will show mercy and abundantly pardon. May we remember that as we diligently work to restore legal protection for the unborn, the disabled, the medically dependent and all innocent children of God whose lives are threatened. And, Lord, grant us peaceful hearts as we labor for life. In Jesus' Name, Amen!

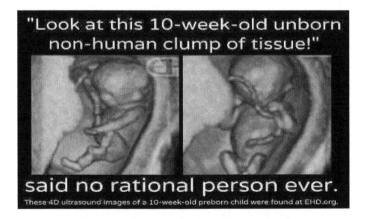

January 27

"Wash yourselves, make yourselves clean; Put away the evil of your doings from before My eyes. Cease to do evil, learn to do good; seek justice, rebuke the oppressor; defend the fatherless, plead for the widow."
(Isaiah 1:16-17)

O God, our heavenly Father, give us courage and wisdom as we seek to eradicate the evil of abortion in our society. Help us to realize that your divine Spirit alone can change hearts and minds so that all your human creatures may enjoy the fullness of life you intended for them. May we see your creative hand at work, even from the very moment of conception. In Jesus' Name, Amen!

January 28

"Woe to those who call evil good, and good evil;
Who put darkness for light, and light for darkness;
Who put bitter for sweet, and sweet for bitter!"
(Isa 5:20 NKJV)

Almighty God, this Scripture is certainly being fulfilled in our time. Call out your people to make the distinction, in our prayers, our words, and our deeds that life is good and murder is evil In Jesus' Name, Amen!

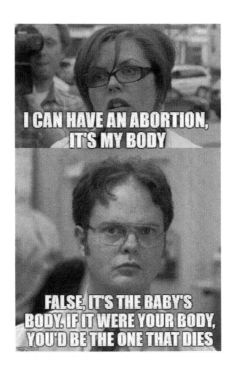

January 29

"If anyone says, 'I love God,' and hates his brother, he is a liar; for he who does not love his brother whom he has seen cannot love God whom he has not seen."
(1John 4:20)

Father, help us to embrace the fact that we are our "brother's keeper." When, due to selfish motives, we try to cast off this responsibility please call to us to account. We would be pleasing to you and to our "brother." And help us to understand that the word "brother" in this context knows no gender, racial or ethnic restrictions. Red and yellow, black and white, male and female, left and right - they are all precious in your sight. They all receive life from you - may we be strong defenders of life. In Jesus' Name, Amen!

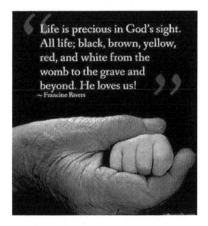

January 30

"Your eyes saw my substance, being yet unformed.
And in Your book they all were written, the days
fashioned for me, when as yet there were none of
them."
(Psalm 139:16)

Gracious God, help us to appreciate the wonder
and beauty of Your creation. Help us proclaim on
behalf of every one of our fellow human beings, "I
am fearfully and wonderfully made." May the
knowledge that we are intimately known by You
shape our lives and actions, that we all might
choose life, both personally, and as one nation
under God. In Jesus' Name, Amen!

"The Child Who was Never Born" by Martin Hudáceka

January 31

"The dragon stood before the woman who was about to give birth, so that when she bore her child he might devour it. She gave birth to a male child, who is to rule all the nations with a rod of iron, but her child was caught up to God and to his throne."
(Revelation 12:4-5)

O God, from generation to generation, you have called your people to be the very aroma of life amidst a culture of death. Now it is our turn. Prepare us. Send us. Use us. We are eager to do our part. Stir your people everywhere to take up this great work so that every human creation might be given a chance to glorify You. In Jesus' Name, Amen!

Graphic represents statistics as of 2014

February 1

"When I consider Your heavens, the work of Your fingers, the moon and the stars, which You have ordained, what is man that You are mindful of him, and the son of man that You visit him? For You have made him a little lower than the angels, and You have crowned him with glory and honor."
(Psalm 8:3-5)

Lord, you are the creator of all things. Guide my thoughts to consider your creation in all of its majesty, beauty and holiness. Guide my heart especially to your creation of precious human life. Help me to comprehend how essential life is in your own heart. Teach me to appreciate, love and protect all human life, even from the moment of conception. In Jesus. Name, Amen!

" hmmm yes, you are correct 10 out of 10 babies prefer life! "

www.911Babies.com

February 2

*"That the God of our Lord Jesus Christ, the Father
of glory, may give unto you the spirit of wisdom
and revelation in the knowledge of him: The eyes
of your understanding being enlightened; that ye
may know what is the hope of his calling, and what
the riches of the glory of his inheritance in the
saints."*
(Ephesians 1:17-18)

Lord we come in agreement, asking that pro-
abortion events promoted by Planned Parenthood
at whatever time or place, billed as "Abortion is
Normal," will be dominated by the Truth of Your
Word. Lord we pray this agenda will be
completely ignored. You hear the leaders saying to
"shout their abortion" as a movement. Father,
forgive them for they know not what they do.
Would You in Your mercy turn their hearts to You
today? Thank You Lord. In Jesus' Name, Amen!

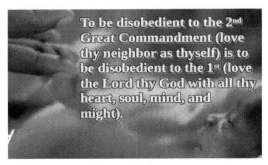

To be disobedient to the 2nd
Great Commandment (love
thy neighbor as thyself) is to
be disobedient to the 1st (love
the Lord thy God with all thy
heart, soul, mind, and
might).

February 3

"Blessed are those whose lawless deeds are forgiven, and whose sin is covered. Blessed is the one to whom the Lord shall not impute sin."
Romans 4:7-8

Most Gracious Heavenly Father, thank you for your amazing grace that saved a wretch like me. I know that your will is that all would come to the knowledge of the truth and be saved. Save those who are bound up in the darkness of abortion and bring them into your marvelous light, that all might be granted the opportunity to live – and that more abundantly. In Jesus' Name, Amen!

Why do some abortionists and the devil understand what the Church is hesitant to acknowledge...?

The devil "...was a murderer from the beginning..." he "...comes only to steal and kill and destroy."
John 8:44; 10:10

An abortionist's prayer
"In my abortionist's hands I hold the plastic-tipped wand attached to a suction machine... May my hands move the wand skillfully, feeling the moment of emptying... May my hands stay connected to my heart as I release this spirit and return this woman to herself and other possibilities."
"Blessings for the Abortionist's Hands" by Elizabeth Moonstone, practicing witch & abortionist who has released 16,000 spirits (unborn babies) since 1991

Abortion is a gospel issue.
The Church for Life

February 4

"Thus says the Lord: 'For three transgressions of the Ammonites, and for four, I will not revoke the punishment, because they have ripped open pregnant women in Gilead, that they might enlarge their border.'"
(Amos 1:13)

O God. We understand that your justice, although it may seem slow in coming to us at times, is always sure and precise. The Ammonites are not the only nation who will have been punished for the sin of genocide. May we become a nation that repents and once again loves you. May we reflect that love by loving your precepts, including "Thou shall not commit murder!" In Jesus' Name. Amen!

February 5

"For the law was given by Moses, but grace and truth came by Jesus Christ."
(John 1:17)

"Jesus saith unto him, 'I am the way, the truth, and the life: no man cometh unto the Father, but by me.'"
(John 14:6)

Even now Lord speak to the hearts of those who feel trapped in their unplanned pregnancies. Show them that life is the better option, including adoption. Thank You that You will make a way for them. We ask that You instill hope along with the knowledge that two wrongs do not a make a right. Today O Lord we pray that lives will be saved, physically and spiritually across the country, and that abortion will come to an end. In Jesus' Name, Amen!

February 6

"You have heard that it was said, 'you shall love your neighbor, and hate your enemy.' But I say to you, love your enemies, bless those who curse you, do good to those who hate you, and pray for those who spitefully use you and persecute you."
(Matthew 5: 43-44)

Heavenly Father, may we reflect your character of grace to those who hate us and curse us, even as we stand firm on the issue of life. Guard our hearts and our tongues as we respond in love and truth to words and actions meant to rile us or cause us harm. Let others see the Hope that is Christ in all we say and do so that all the victims may truly experience life. In Jesus' Name, Amen!

February 7

"In this you greatly rejoice, though now for a little while, if need be, you have been grieved by various trials, that the genuineness of your faith, being much more precious than gold that perishes, though it is tested by fire, may be found to praise, honor and glory at the revelation of Jesus Christ."
(1 Peter 1:6-7)

Dear Heavenly Father, we sing to You a new song, for You have done marvelous things. Forgive us when we allow circumstances to weary us. You give power to the faint and You increase strength in those who have no might. We rest in You dear Lord, and ask You to empower us for Your service as we work to bring about an end to legal abortion. In Jesus' Name, Amen!

February 8

"He will wipe every tear from their eyes. There will be no more death or mourning or crying or pain, for the old order of things has passed away. He who was seated on the throne said, 'I am making everything new!'"
(Revelation 21:4-5)

Father, you are the God of hope. Your word fills us with the vision of the world to come, when every tear will be wiped away, and death will be no more. Father, we need that hope; we are strengthened by that vision! Keep our hearts focused on heaven, and diligent in the labors of earth. Abortion doesn't take a vacation, so we continue the fight against the culture of death. Our prayers and actions for the end of abortion go on until there is justice for the unborn in our nation again. In Jesus' Name, Amen!

February 9

"...therefore, as I live, declares the Lord God, I will prepare you for blood, and blood shall pursue you; because you did not hate bloodshed, therefore blood shall pursue you."
Ezekiel 35:6

One Christian pro-life missionary has said repeatedly: "If America does not Repent and END child-murder, we as a country will be judged calamitously with a national bloodbath for this national sin, just as America was judged (both North and South) in 1861-1865, for the national sin and bloodshed of un-Biblical American Slavery, when 600,000 - 700,000 died in the War Between Americans which God gave to both North and South."

Lord, You have said that judgment begins in the house of the Lord. May we truly repent of our apathy and indifference, so that we may experience the blessing of mercy triumphing over judgment. In Jesus' Name, Amen!

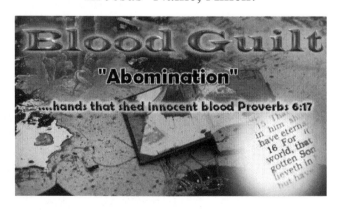

February 10

"Your eye shall not pity him, but you shall put away the guilt of innocent blood from Israel, that it may go well with you."
(Deuteronomy 19:13)

Father, we recognize that the shedding of innocent blood has always been a personal sin, and that when a nation condones it, it becomes a national sin. Because silence is considered approval, the church is complicit in this sin as well. As we confess our sins in this area, may we also find grace to repent, and to be silent no more. In Jesus' Name, Amen!

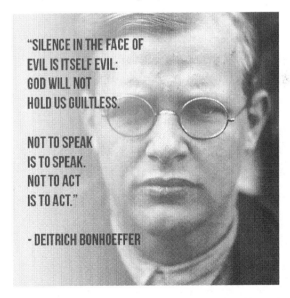

February 11

"Now there was a man in Jerusalem, whose name was Simeon, and this man was righteous and devout... and the Holy Spirit was upon him. And it had been revealed to him by the Holy Spirit that he would not see death before he had seen the Lord's Christ." (Luke 2:25-26)

Heavenly Father, we see from your Holy Word and from history that you always bring about salvation, deliverance, revival and reformation through the womb, through a baby. Thank you for Moses, Jonathan Edwards, Martin Luther, John Newton, and most of all, thank you for Jesus. Jesus, may we honor You in our fight for life. In Your Name we pray, Amen!

Not a mistake
Not a problem
Not a burden
Not an inconvenience
Not a nuisance
Not an accident
Not a punishment

A miracle

February 12

"Before I formed you in the womb I knew you, and before you were born I consecrated you; I appointed you a prophet to the nations."
(Jeremiah 1:5)

Father God, we realize that each of us was created for a purpose even before you formed us in our mother's womb. Help us to help others reach their intended purpose, even from the moment of conception. Remove the deception of abortion being portrayed as a right to privacy. In Jesus' Name, Amen!

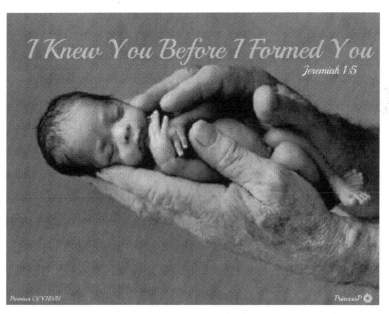

February 13

"But when he who had set me apart before I was born , and who called me by his grace..."
(Galatians 1:15)

Father, this side of eternity we will never know how many plans and purposes of yours were cancelled because of murder in the womb. Yet we trust that ultimately even all this will ultimately be used for your glory. In the meantime, may we not grow weary in our defense of the gift of life. In Jesus' Name, Amen!

February 14

"You created my inmost being; You knit me together in my mother's womb..Your eyes saw my unformed body. All the days ordained for me were written in Your book before one of them came to be."
(Psalm 139:13, 16)

Father, forgive us for not trusting you with the days of our lives, and for allowing that distrust to spill over into other areas where we choose to make the life and death decisions, that affect babies, mothers, and fathers. Help us to always choose life. In Jesus' Name, Amen!

Abortion is not just a women issue, it affects the hearts of the fathers as well.

www.godeeperstill.org

February 15

"Your hands shaped me and made me... Did You not clothe me with skin and flesh and knit me together with bones and sinews? You gave me life."
(Job 10:8, 11, 12)

Heavenly Father, we who have been birthed into the life you have planned for us intercede in behalf of those whose lives will be subjected to plots of death today. Grant the grace of repentance to all who would be involved in such atrocities. In Jesus' Name, Amen!

February 16

"Thus says the Lord who made you, who formed you from the womb and will help you: Fear not, O Jacob my servant, Jeshurun whom I have chosen."
(Isaiah 44:2)

Dear Lord, it is You who made us and not we ourselves. May we bow our knees to your Lordship and treat every life, from conception to natural death with respect and dignity. For those with no voice, empower us to be their voice. In Jesus' Name, Amen!

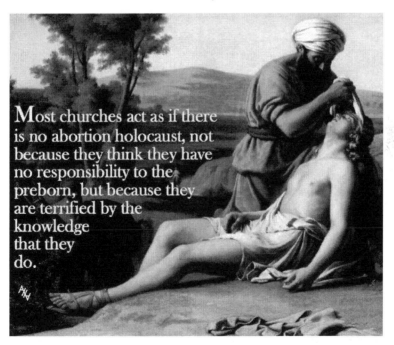

Most churches act as if there is no abortion holocaust, not because they think they have no responsibility to the preborn, but because they are terrified by the knowledge that they do.

February 17

"Did not he who made me in the womb make him?
And did not one fashion us in the womb?"
(Job 31:15)

Oh God! In this so-called age of enlightenment, please grant us the wisdom of the ancients. May all people come to the knowledge that You are our creator, and that every life is precious. May the wombs of mothers cease to be places of destruction and death. In Jesus' Name. Amen!

Four decades of abortion on demand
has defaced America.

rememberingroe.com

As of 2018 – 4-1/2 decades and 6 million more deaths

February 18

"So God created man in his own image, in the image of God he created him; male and female he created them."
(Genesis 1:27)

Because each one of us is made in your image, O God, each one of us is valuable and precious. That includes every baby in the womb, from the moment of conception. May the laws of this country reflect that truth, without further delay. In Jesus' Name, Amen!

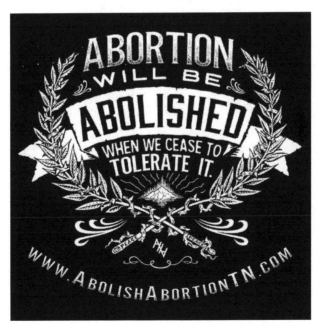

February 19

"Behold, children are a heritage from the Lord, the fruit of the womb a reward."
(Psalms 127:3)

Father, forgive us for despising and rejecting 60+ million of these rewards. May the truth, which is in Christ, deliver us from all lies, and may the life which is in Christ deliver us from this culture of death. For it is in His Name we pray, Amen!

February 20

"And you took your sons and your daughters, whom you had borne to me, and these you sacrificed to them to be devoured. Were your whorings so small a matter that you slaughtered my children and delivered them up as an offering by fire to them?"
(Ezekiel 16:20-21)

Most High God, you even call our children "Your children." How arrogant and presumptuous we are to take your innocent, little ones and sacrifice them to the gods of convenience and pride. Forgive us individually and as a nation, for having "legalized" this sin. Grant us repentance, in Jesus' Name, Amen!

February 21

"In his hand is the life of every living thing and the breath of all mankind."
(Job 12:10)

O God! When we decide to end a life outside of your parameters, we are guilty of presuming to be God. Forgive us of our arrogance and pride. There is no justification for such action. May we become again "one nation under God," acknowledging you as the Lord, the giver of life, from conception until natural death. In Jesus' Name, Amen!

February 22

"If you do not... shed innocent blood in this place, and if you do not go after other gods to your own harm,"
(Jeremiah 7:6)

Heavenly Father, there is no blood more innocent than that of the pre-born baby in the womb. The amount of that bloodshed in this land, under protection of quasi-law, is staggering. Lord, may the church rise up with a unified voice and demand an end to the genocide, NOW! In Jesus' Name! Amen!

February 23

" 'Cursed be anyone who takes a bribe to shed innocent blood.' And all the people shall say, 'Amen.'"
(Deuteronomy 27:25)

Most High God, doctors and Planned Parenthood taking payments for abortions meet this criteria; thus they are cursed, according to your word. Only Jesus Christ can redeem one from the curse of the Law. May His lordship, proclaimed by His church, put an end to the genocide. In Jesus' Name, Amen!

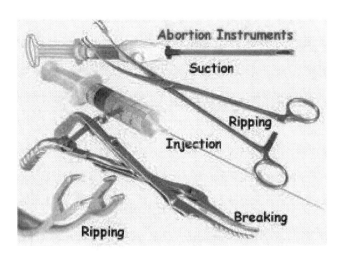

February 24

"You shall not murder."
(Exodus 20:13)

Father, forgive us for not just committing murder, but in the case of the unborn, for legalizing and facilitating it. Your church has been silent and apathetic. Grant us grace to repent in our hearts and in our actions, in Jesus' Name, Amen!

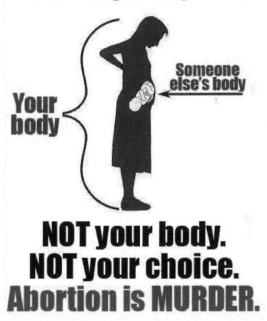

February 25

"...because he did not kill me in the womb; so my mother would have been my grave..."
(Jeremiah 20:17)

Dear Lord, we can see clearly from your Word that killing babies in the womb is murder. It is an abomination to You - the Lord and giver of life. Help us to bring an end to the genocide in our country. Cause the 3.1.10 Initiative* to go viral, and for Congress to respond accordingly. In Jesus' Name. Amen!

ABORTION IS NOT A POLITICAL ISSUE. ABORTION IS THE INTENTIONAL MURDER OF A CHILD BY HIS OR HER PARENTS

PERSONHOOD.COM

*See Epilogue for 3.1.10 Initiative details

February 26

"When men strive together and hit a pregnant woman, so that her children come out, but there is no harm, the one who hit her shall... be fined... and he shall pay as the judges determine. But if there is harm, then you shall pay life for life,"
(Exodus 21:22-23)

Lord God, it is obvious from your eternal Word that the baby in the womb is human life, worth every bit as much as outside the womb. Show our country the error of its ways in legalizing abortion and help us to restore a righteous foundation. In Jesus' Name, Amen!

February 27

"I call heaven and earth to witness against you today, that I have set before you life and death, blessing and curse. Therefore choose life, that you and your offspring may live,"
(Deuteronomy 30:19)

Father God, thank you for making us with the ability to make choices. It is obvious that you choose life. Convict and empower us to choose life as well, both as individuals and as a nation. We have dug ourselves into a pit and we need you to help us out. In Jesus' Name, Amen!

February 28

"There are six things that the Lord hates, seven that are an abomination to him: 17 haughty eyes, a lying tongue, and hands that shed innocent blood, 18 a heart that devises wicked plans, feet that make haste to run to evil, 19 a false witness who breathes out lies, and one who sows discord among brothers."
(Proverbs 6:16-19)

Almighty God, if the shedding of innocent blood is an abomination to You, how much more a nation that condones and legalizes the practice. If there is still time for the grace of repentance to be given, let it be according to your mercy, In Jesus' Name, Amen!

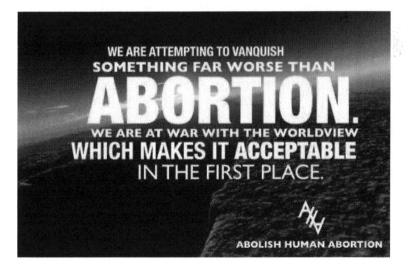

March 1

"...For the life of a creature is in the blood..."
(Leviticus 17:11)

Father, we understand from experience that every abortion involves the shedding of blood and your word tells us that life is in the blood. We stand guilty of the shedding of innocent blood (life). How far we have fallen from "One Nation Under God." Have mercy on us we pray. In Jesus' Name, Amen!

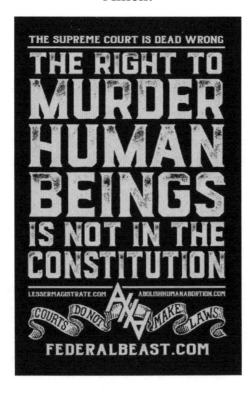

March 2

"Show him no pity. You must purge from Israel the guilt of shedding innocent blood, so that it may go well with you."
(Deuteronomy 19:13)

Almighty God, only your mercy has kept our nation from judgment. It is obvious that all is not going well with our country, and we confess that abortion and our complicity/apathy in that matter is probably a root cause. Grant us the motivation and strength to restore righteousness to our land. In Jesus' Name, Amen!

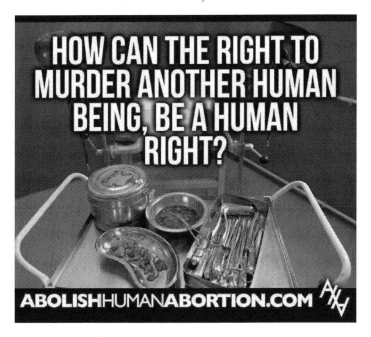

March 3

"He will rescue them from oppression and violence, for precious is their blood in His sight."
(Psalm 72:14)

Father God, thank you for helping us to see precious little ones in the womb through your eyes. May we, as a nation, return to the place where we consider them precious, and worthy of every protection under the law. May we, as Your church, pray and work hard toward that end... In Jesus' Name, Amen!

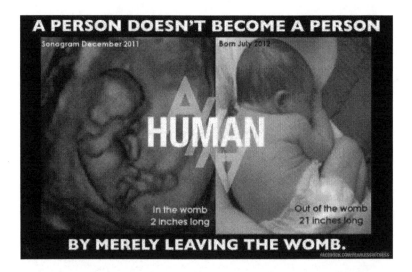

March 4

*"And a second is like it: You shall love your
neighbor as yourself."*
(Matthew 22:39)

Father, help us to recognize that babies in the
womb are also our neighbors, no less than their
mothers and fathers. The difference is they have no
voice; they are helpless. So help us to love them,
not just in our words and prayers, but in deeds and
actions. In Jesus' Name, Amen!

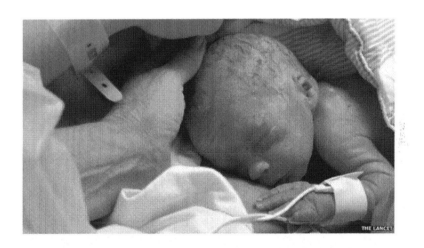

March 5

"You shall not pollute the land in which you live, for blood pollutes the land, and no atonement can be made for the land for the blood that is shed in it, except by the blood of the one who shed it."
(Numbers 35:33)

Most High God, our land has become polluted with the blood of innocent babies. Only your mercy and the grace of our Lord Jesus Christ can bring about repentance and a restoration of righteousness. May Your love expressed through Your church cause it to happen before it is too late, in Jesus' Name, Amen!

Abortion says, "I sacrifice the other person for the good of myself."
Love says, "I sacrifice myself for the good of the other person."

March 6

"They sacrificed their sons and their daughters to the demons; they poured out innocent blood, the blood of their sons and daughters, whom they sacrificed to the idols of Canaan, and the land was polluted with blood."
(Psalm 106:37-38)

Father, forgive our arrogance, pride, and rebellion. We proclaim ourselves as "great" and yet we engage in the barbaric practice of child sacrifice. Your church hardly utters a whimper in protest. Grant us hearts of repentance that healing might come to our land. In Jesus' Name. Amen!

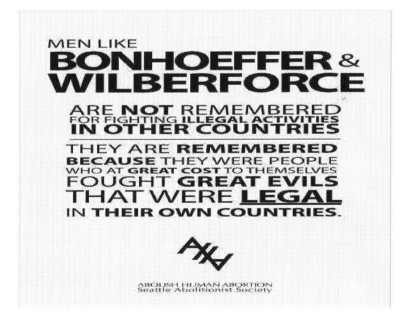

MEN LIKE
BONHOEFFER & **WILBERFORCE**
ARE **NOT** REMEMBERED FOR FIGHTING ILLEGAL ACTIVITIES **IN OTHER COUNTRIES**
THEY ARE **REMEMBERED BECAUSE** THEY WERE PEOPLE WHO AT **GREAT COST** TO THEMSELVES FOUGHT **GREAT EVILS** THAT WERE **LEGAL** IN **THEIR OWN COUNTRIES**.

ABOLISH HUMAN ABORTION
Seattle Abolitionist Society

March 7

"...and also for the innocent blood that he [Manasseh] had shed. For he filled Jerusalem with innocent blood, and the LORD would not pardon."
(2 Kings 24:4)

Most High God, Possessor of Heaven and Earth, have we as a nation gone too far? Have we gone the way of Manasseh, beyond pardon? O Lord, we plead for your mercy, and for the grace to repent as a nation. May our laws reflect your view of life, even life in the womb. In Jesus' Name, Amen!

March 8

"... on your skirts is found the lifeblood of the guiltless poor; you did not find them breaking in. Yet in spite of all these things you say, 'I am innocent; surely his anger has turned from me.' Behold, I will bring you to judgment for saying, 'I have not sinned.'"
(Jeremiah 2:33-35)

Heavenly Father, we set our hearts to view things as You do. By your grace, no longer shall we rationalize or excuse what you call sin. The shedding of innocent blood (including that of babies in the womb) is a sin, from which we must repent. Even we who have not committed the deed but have stood idly by are guilty. Forgive us we plead, in Jesus' Name, Amen!

March 9

"...lest innocent blood be shed in your land that the LORD your God is giving you for an inheritance, and so the guilt of bloodshed be upon you."
(Deuteronomy 19:10)

Holy God, if you declare us guilty, then we are indeed guilty. Yours is the highest court in all of creation. We confess our sins, both personally and nationally; then we appeal to you for mercy, through our Advocate, the Lord Jesus Christ, Amen!

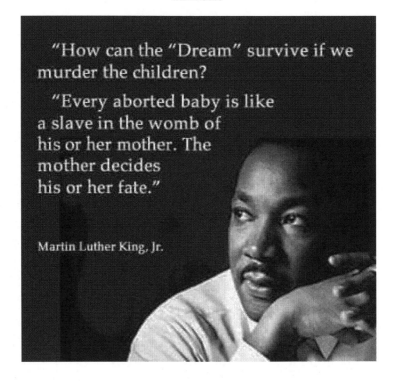

"How can the "Dream" survive if we murder the children?

"Every aborted baby is like a slave in the womb of his or her mother. The mother decides his or her fate."

Martin Luther King, Jr.

"Behold, children are a heritage from the LORD, the fruit of the womb a reward. Like arrows in the hand of a warrior are the children of one's youth. Blessed is the man who fills his quiver with them! He shall not be put to shame when he speaks with his enemies in the gate."
(Psalm 127:3-5)

Heavenly Father, you are good, good, good! Help us to pattern our parenthood after yours. Help us to intellectually, affectionately, and legally value life in all its stages, and to consider children as the blessings which you declare. In Jesus' Name, Amen!

March 11

*"And when Elizabeth heard the greeting of Mary,
the baby leaped in her womb. And Elizabeth was
filled with the Holy Spirit,"*
(Luke 1:41)

Father God, we see from Your Word that babies
experience emotions, while yet in the womb. You
make it clear, and science affirms, that babies are
people - little human beings. Open our eyes to that
fact so that the genocide may cease to be a legal
choice. In Jesus' Name, Amen!

March 12

"And Mary said to the angel, 'How will this be, since I am a virgin?' And the angel answered her, 'The Holy Spirit will come upon you, and the power of the Most High will overshadow you; therefore the child to be born will be called holy-- the Son of God.'"
(Luke1:34-35)

Father God, thank you for the grace to understand that from a human perspective, a pregnancy may be unplanned; but from your perspective, every one is planned and has a purpose. May life triumph over death in our land, in Jesus' Name. Amen!

March 13

"And he will turn many of the children of Israel to the Lord their God, and he will go before him in the spirit and power of Elijah, to turn the hearts of the fathers to the children, and the disobedient to the wisdom of the just, to make ready for the Lord a people prepared."
(Luke 1:16-17)

Holy God, You are the One who sees the end from the beginning. Our finite minds have no idea of what great purpose you may have created a human life. For that reason each one has a unique and specific value. Grant us the grace to trust you and not take things into our own fallible hands. In Jesus' Name. Amen!

March 14

"And Jesus increased in wisdom and stature, and in favor with God and man."
(Luke 2:52)

Lord - help us to realize that every person, from the moment of conception, should be given the opportunity to "increase in wisdom and stature, and in favor with You and man." Help our culture to reflect the fact that life is precious, even in its beginning forms. In Jesus' Name. Amen!

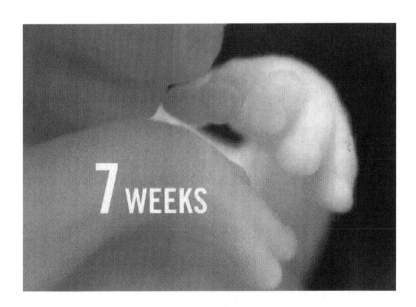

March 15

"Now the birth of Jesus Christ took place in this way. When his mother Mary had been betrothed to Joseph, before they came together she was found to be with child from the Holy Spirit. And her husband Joseph, being a just man and unwilling to put her to shame, resolved to divorce her quietly."
(Matthew 1:18-19)

Heavenly Father, we see that even the plan of a just and compassionate man like Joseph was not your plan for Mary and the baby in her womb. The redemptive plan of God was hidden within an unplanned, unexpected, inconvenient pregnancy. Forgive us for the many times we think we know better than You. Help us all to be defenders of human life. In Jesus' Name, Amen!

March 16

"...and also for the innocent blood that he had shed. For he filled Jerusalem with innocent blood, and the Lord would not pardon."
(2 Kings 24:4)

Holy God, only You know whether we, like Manasseh in days of old, have gone past the point of pardon. So we yield to both your justice and your mercy. May this be the year in which your church arises and says, with one voice, "No more abortion!" In Jesus' Name, Amen!

FRANCIS SCHAEFFER, ABORTION ABOLITIONIST — NO COMPROMISE. ABOLISH HUMAN ABORTION.

"IN FRONT OF EVERY ABORTION CLINIC THERE NEEDS TO BE A SIGN THAT READS, HERE BY PERMISSION OF THE CHURCH."

March 17

"Then Herod, when he saw that he had been tricked by the wise men, became furious, and he sent and killed all the male children in Bethlehem and in all that region who were two years old or under, according to the time that he had ascertained from the wise men."
(Matthew 2:16)

Omniscient God, You who know the end from the beginning; we confess that every time anyone takes the life of an innocent little one (from the moment of conception on) it is an attempt to raise human will and authority over Yours. You have a purpose for every life. Forgive us and grant us grace to bend our knees to your will. In Jesus' Name, Amen!

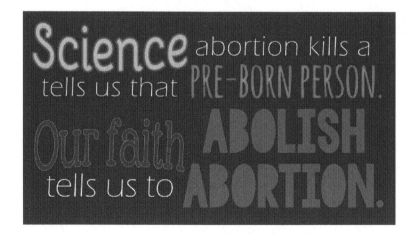

March 18

"You have cut short the days of his youth; you have covered him with shame. Selah"
(Psalm 89:45)

Father God, we pray that every child, from the moment of conception on would be given the opportunity to live out their full life, according to the days written in Your Book, being allowed to fulfill Your purpose for them. In Jesus' Name, Amen!

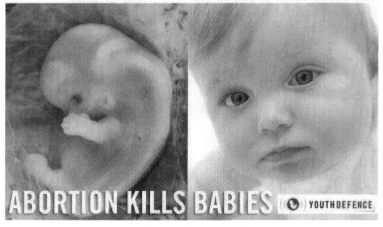

March 19

"And she named the child Ichabod, saying, 'The glory has departed from Israel!'"
(1 Samuel 4:21a)

Lord God, we pray that the peace of God which transcends all understanding will keep each of our hearts and minds in Christ Jesus. We also pray that our status-quo peace is disturbed to the point where we accomplish more in behalf of "the least of these." Let not our contentment become laziness or apathy. Help us bring an end to legalized abortion in our country and help us prepare for all that precedes the return of Christ. Be glorified, Lord, in our lives. In Jesus' Name, Amen!

March 20

*"It is [our] eager expectation and hope that [we]
will not be at all ashamed, but that with full
courage now as always Christ will be honored..."*
(Philippians 1:20)

In the past, at least two presidents (Jackson and
Lincoln) have issued executive orders defying
Supreme Court rulings. Father, while we pray that
our president might have the courage to take a
strong stand for the sanctity of life, beginning at
the moment of conception, we also pray that we
would stand courageously in that battle as well. In
Jesus' Name, Amen!

The care of human life and happiness,
and not their destruction, is the first and
only object of good government.
Thomas Jefferson

March 21

"And the LORD said to him, 'Pass through the city, through Jerusalem, and put a mark on the foreheads of the men who sigh and groan over all the abominations that are committed in it.'"
(Ezekiel 9:4)

Sovereign Lord, you make it clear in Your Word that it is possible for a nation to go beyond the point of no return. We pray today that America would still have time to repent of the genocide that has been legalized for 46 years. If it's too late, we are grateful for your mercy towards those who sigh and groan because of the abominations. Hear our cries O Lord, attend unto our prayers, in Jesus' Name, Amen!

March 22

"Since we have the same spirit of faith according to what has been written, 'I believed, and so I spoke," we also believe, and so we also speak'"
(2 Corinthians 4:13)

The only voice that doesn't count is the one that doesn't speak.

Father, help the church to realize that she has a powerful voice if she would only use it. Prompt us to speak out in defense of those who have no voice; help us speak life in behalf of those doomed to death. Remind us to call our congressmen at least once a month and demand Personhood/Life at Conception legislation. In Jesus' Name, Amen!

"The silent and dormant church is the abortion industry's biggest ally. The abortion holocaust would end overnight if just a fraction of the nation's 500,000 churches became active in the fight."
- Mark Crutcher, Life Dynamics

March 23

"Righteousness exalts a nation, but sin is a reproach to any people."
(Proverbs 14:34)

Father God - we cry out to you today in anguish over the abominable 46 year history of legalized genocide in our country. May our cries also reach the halls of Congress resulting in passage of a Personhood law that once again restores righteousness to our foundations. In Jesus' Name, Amen!

"In America, we are sinking because of very poor policy, the worst of which is legalized genocide of 60 million babies in the womb. That's a crumbling foundation that no amount of kitchen remodeling can fix." -Les Young

March 24

"And should not I pity Nineveh, that great city, in which there are more than 120,000 persons who do not know their right hand from their left, and also much cattle?"
(Jonah 4:11)

Heavenly Father, we see that in the wicked city of Nineveh there were 120,000 little ones below the age of reason. You took pit on the city, they repented, and all were spared. May we repent as well, replacing legal abortion with Personhood legislation. In Jesus' Name, Amen!

March 25

"And it happened, when Elizabeth heard the greeting of Mary that the babe leaped in her womb; and Elizabeth was filled with the Holy Spirit. She spoke out with a loud voice and said, 'Blessed are you among women, and blessed is the fruit of your womb! But why is this granted to me, that the mother of my Lord should come to me?"
(Luke 1:41-44)

Jesus, as some in Your church celebrate the Annunciation, may we all experience hearts of joy over the pending birth of every child. As you experienced human life in the womb of Mary, may every child still in the womb be granted the same opportunity. Grant to all expectant mothers strength and joy as they welcome the gift of life. In Your Name we pray, Amen!

THE FIRST PERSON TO RECOGNIZE JESUS

WAS AN UNBORN CHILD
LUKE 1:41

March 26

"But Peter and the apostles answered, "We must obey God rather than men."
(Act 5:29)

Heavenly Father, may men and women of principled courage rise up and declare "No more murder of innocents in the womb." Restore righteous law and judgment to our land, in Jesus' Name, Amen!

March 27

"Only know for certain that if you put me to death, you will bring innocent blood upon yourselves and upon this city and its inhabitants, for in truth the LORD sent me to you to speak all these words in your ears."
(Jeremiah 26:15)

Father God, open the eyes of the blind; open the ears of the deaf; give voice to the mute; give courage to the coward; give a sense of importance to the apathetic; and give a sense of urgency to the complacent. So that the genocide would end in the very near future, we ask this in Jesus' Name, Amen!

46 years and counting; 60-65 million dead. Have we become deaf to the cries of the voiceless? How can this be in a nation that acknowledges life as an inalienable right, endowed to all by our Creator? -Les Young

March 28

"Ephraim has given bitter provocation; so his Lord will leave his bloodguilt on him and will repay him for his disgraceful deeds."
(Hosea 12:14)

Almighty God, if it were not for your lovingkindness, we would have been consumed already. We understand that judgment is yours to give, either by stretching out your hand in justice, or removing your hand of merciful protection. We pray for mercy, while submitting to your will, as we fight to defend the life of the innocent. In Jesus' Name, Amen!

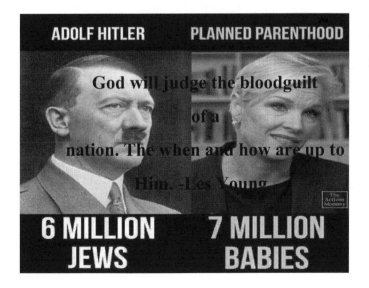

March 29

"Before I formed you in the womb I knew you, and before you were born I consecrated you; I appointed you a prophet to the nations."
(Jeremiah 1:5)

Heavenly Father, your Word makes it abundantly clear that human life begins at conception. Thank you for a Florida law that recognizes that when death of an unborn baby is caused by abortifacients administered by stealth of force, it is considered a crime of violence. May our nation wake up to the sanctity of life, seeing it through your eyes. In Jesus' Name, Amen!

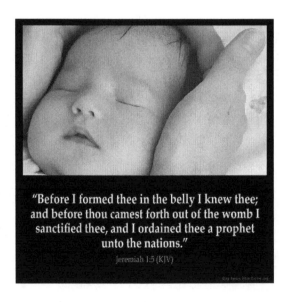

"Before I formed thee in the belly I knew thee; and before thou camest forth out of the womb I sanctified thee, and I ordained thee a prophet unto the nations."

Jeremiah 1:5 (KJV)

March 30

Perez was born of a woman (Tamar) who became pregnant by posing as a prostitute and having intercourse with her father-in-law (Judah). Perez was a "trick baby" (Genesis 38). Yet Perez is in the lineage of Jesus the Christ (Matthew 1:3). Every life is valuable.

Heavenly Father, help us to see that abortion is not a health-care measure that should be regulated, or a human rights issue that should be protected. Your Word makes it clear that it is murder – the shedding of innocent blood, and as such should be abolished. Give us the grace to repent, personally and nationally. In Jesus' Name, Amen!

https://www.facebook.com/joshua.feuerstein.5/videos/599919886777364/

March 31

"...the Lord hates... hands that shed innocent blood,"
(Proverbs 6:16-17)

Father God, many of those engaged in the fight to end abortion decry the actions of the US Congress which, for 46 years has refused the support any bill which would recognize Personhood and due process as applying to babies in the womb. Help us press on until all genocide of the pre-born is ended and Personhood status applies to all - from the moment of conception. In Jesus' Name, Amen!

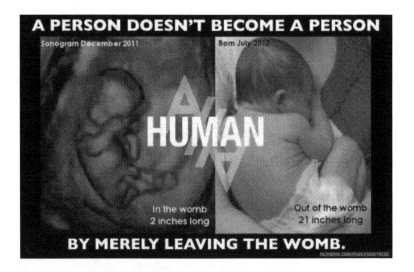

PRAY FOR THE UNBORN: Our National Sin

Pray for our neighbors
Our sisters and brothers
Especially these babes
Betrayed by their mothers

The same God that made us
Also made them (Job 31:15).
Pray for an end
To this national sin

We pray for these things
With no hint of shame
We pray for these babes
In Christ's holy name (John 14:14)

They cut them to pieces
And burn of their skins (Micah 3:2,3.)
And then celebrate
This national sin

These brutal acts
Should move men to tears(Jeremiah 9:1)
But since 73
It seems no one cares

So, pray for these babes
Again and again
One day we'll be judged
For this national sin

Linen, M. (2018). Death Roe: State Funded Racism, Torture, and Murder.
Unpublished manuscript.

April 1

"The thief comes only to steal and kill and destroy. I came that they may have life and have it abundantly."
(John 10:10)

Dear Elohim, help us to see clearly that death is of the enemy and life is of You, the maker of heaven and earth. While death remains an enemy yet to be conquered completely, we have no business pronouncing death sentences upon the smallest, the most innocent, and the most defenseless of our citizens. Help us to abolish human abortion in our nation, in Jesus' Name, Amen!

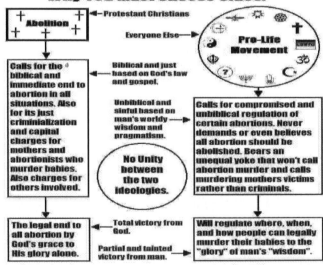

April 2

"For behold, when the sound of your greeting came to my ears, the baby in my womb leaped for joy." (Luke 1:44)

"I tell you, among those born of women none is greater than John. Yet the one who is least in the kingdom of God is greater than he." (Luke 7:28)

Father God, we understand from your Word that the greatest prophet ever born by natural birth alone was John the Baptist. We also understand that while yet in his mother's womb that he responded to the voice of Mary, who at the time was carrying Jesus in her womb. Help us, as a nation and as your church, to see that life in the womb is precious, even from the moment of conception; hence it should be protected by our laws rather than being set up for legal extermination. In Jesus' Name, Amen!

April 3

"Yet you are he who took me from the womb; you made me trust you at my mother's breasts. On you was I cast from my birth, and from my mother's womb you have been my God."
(Psalm 22:9-10)

Father God, we see in your Word that life in the womb is your doing. You have a plan for every life. Forgive us for being so presumptuous to think that we have a right to interrupt those plans by determining that some lives are not worth living. Forgive us our apathy in not doing all we can to end such abominable practices. Stir your church to action, in Jesus' Name, Amen!

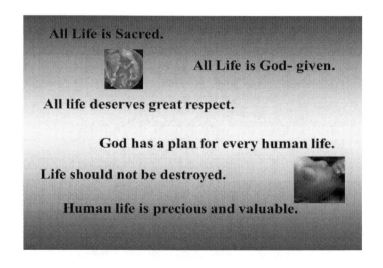

April 4

"It would be better for him if a millstone were hung around his neck, and he were thrown into the sea, than that he should offend one of these little ones."
(Luke 17:2 NKJV)

Heavenly Father, every passed budget bill imperils the USA, both economically and spiritually, when it continues to fund our national sin...abortion. Righteousness has been removed from the land and lies have replaced truth. Raise up a people who still love the truth and will speak it whether it's convenient or not. In Jesus' Name, Amen!

April 5

*"So it is not the will of my Father who is in heaven
that one of these little ones should perish."*
(Matthew 18:14 ESV)

Lord God, help us to step out of the comfortable
gray shadows and be the light that you have called
us to be. Help us to speak with a loud and clear
voice against legalized abortion, while lending
hands and hearts to those who find themselves in
crisis mode over the pending birth of a child. May
there be a clear distinction between what we are
for and what we are against. In Jesus' Name,
Amen!

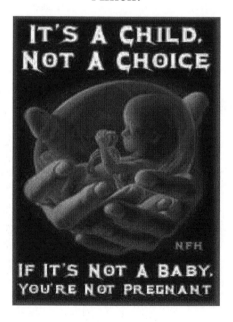

April 6

"Blow the trumpet in Zion! Proclaim a fast, call an assembly. Gather the people, notify the congregation. Assemble the elders; gather the children and the infants at the breast ... Let the priests, the ministers of the Lord, weep and say, "Spare, O Lord, your people."
(Joel 2:15-17)

Lord, we ask for the strength, courage, wisdom, determination and stamina to carry out this mission according to Your will. Help us to not be satisfied with regulated abortion, but to strive for Personhood Law to be enacted. Guide us, we pray, as we go forth and proclaim Your truth. In Jesus' Name, Amen!

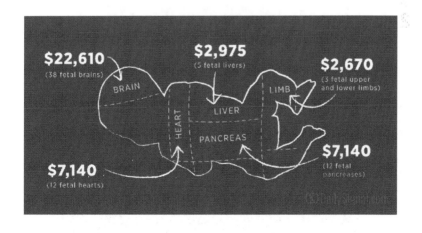

April 7

"Behold, I will send you Elijah the prophet before the great and awesome day of the Lord comes. And he will turn the hearts of fathers to their children and the hearts of children to their fathers, lest I come and strike the land with a decree of utter destruction."
(Malachi 4:5-6)

Lord, we pray for fathers' hearts to turn to their children; to nurture, protect and defend them and consider it unthinkable to bring them to be aborted. Even as the Day of the Lord comes and will come according to your own counsel, may we even then, by our repentance, find mercy. We are so thankful that our Father is a good, good Father. In Jesus' Name, Amen!

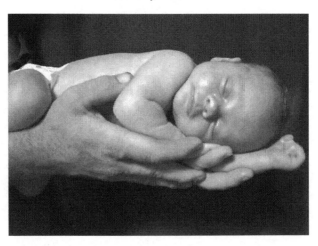

April 8

*"Therefore I tell you, do not worry about your life,
what you will eat or drink; or about your body,
what you will wear. Is not life more important than
food, and the body more important than clothes?
Look at the birds of the air; they do not sow or
reap or store away in barns, and yet your heavenly
Father feeds them. Are you not much more
valuable than they?"*
(Matthew 6:25-26)

Loving heavenly Father, help us to see the worth
of all human beings by the way in which you
provide for us. We would ask that you provide also
the faith, grace and courage to enable us to protect
that which is so precious to you, by our prayers,
our witness, and our laws. In Jesus' Name, Amen!

**Eu-phem-a-sia, noun:
Perpetuating the
genocide of preborns by
employing euphemism to
lessen the heinousness
of murder-by-abortion.**

April 9

*"And the Word became flesh and dwelt among us,
and we have seen his glory, glory as of the only
Son from the Father, full of grace and truth."*
(John 1:14)

Heavenly Father, you have made the womb of
each woman a very special place. Help us to hold
fast to the sanctity of this first home of humanity,
remembering the wonderful mystery - that God
inhabited the womb of a young woman and came
forth as the savior and deliverer of the world. In
Jesus' Name, Amen!

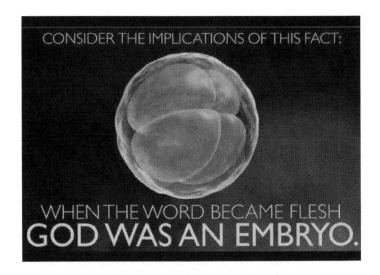

CONSIDER THE IMPLICATIONS OF THIS FACT:

WHEN THE WORD BECAME FLESH
GOD WAS AN EMBRYO.

April 10

*"The King will answer and say to them,
'Assuredly, I say to you, inasmuch as you did it to
one of the least of these my brethren, you did it to
me.'"*
(Matthew 25:31-46)

Gracious and merciful Father, we renew our
dedication to defending the unborn and all whose
right to life is compromised by our godless
society's selfish lack of concern. Free us from our
own failures and sins so that we will be truly pro-
life in every area of our lives. In Jesus' Name,
Amen!

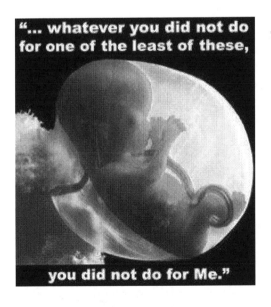

April 11

"Remember your Creator before the silver cord is loosed, or the golden bowl is broken, or the pitcher shattered at the fountain, or the wheel broken at the well. Then the dust will return to the earth as it was, and the spirit will return to God who gave it."
(Ecclesiastes 12:6-7)

O God, too often we live in ways that ignore our coming death. Forgetting that our days are numbered by Youand that at the end of our days your judgment awaits, we live as though we were masters of our own destiny. Help us to repent daily, to live in joyful obedience. Keep our eyes on the light and promise of eternity as we live fully and sacrificially, engaging the culture of death with the life of the Gospel. In Jesus' Name, Amen!

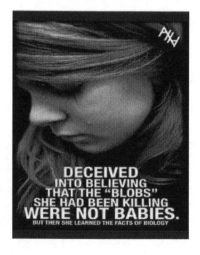

April 12

"For as many of you as were baptized into Christ have put on Christ. 28 There is neither Jew nor Greek, there is neither slave nor free, there is neither male nor female, for you are all one in Christ Jesus."

(Galatians 3:27-28)

Lord, as we labor to abolish abortion and to establish equal protection and justice for babies in the womb, help us to also root out all manner of prejudice in our hearts.Help us to bring healing, liberty, and justice to all, through Jesus Christ our Lord, Amen!

April 13

"Give justice to the weak and the fatherless; maintain the right of the afflicted and the destitute."

Psalms 82:3 (ESV)

Father, give strength today to those serving in our pregnancy resource centers. Grant every worker, from those answering calls to those providing ultrasound a bold spirit of truth, love and perseverance. Grant the sidewalk counselors to know how to speak the truth in love, without sacrificing either. And may all intercessors be empowered by your Spirit to travail and to see results in this fight for life. In Jesus' Name, Amen!

April 14

"I beseech you to walk worthy of the calling with which you were called, with all lowliness, and gentleness, with longsuffering, bearing with one another in love."
(Ephesians 4:1b-2)

Dear Heavenly Father, we are humbled that you have called us and appointed us to be ambassadors of Christ in a world that is not our home. We pray that your Holy Spirit will empower us to walk worthy of our calling. We pray that Your unconditional love will flow through us to those who desperately need Your saving grace, empowering them to choose life rather than death. In Jesus' Name, Amen!

April 15

"Jesus declared, 'Greater love has no one than this, than to lay down one's life for his friends.'" (John 15:13).

Lord God, stir up your church to understand that literally giving up one's life for the victims of abortion would probably not accomplish much. However, if we were to present ourselves as living sacrifices, giving 3-4 minutes a month to call our congressmen demanding passage of Personhood legislation, or giving 2 hours a week to pray and witness at a local abortuary, or volunteering at a crisis pregnancy center, there is no telling what you could accomplish through us. Help us to be silent and inactive no more. In Jesus' Name, Amen!

April 16

"A father of the fatherless, a defender of widows, is God in His holy habitation."
(Psalm 68:5)

Heavenly Father, we thank you for caring about each of us so deeply. Help us to see and know you as our Father in heaven each and every day of our lives. May your loving hand also rest upon every child today carried in its mother's womb. May they be born into this world and come to know fully and personally your endless love. In Jesus' Name, Amen!

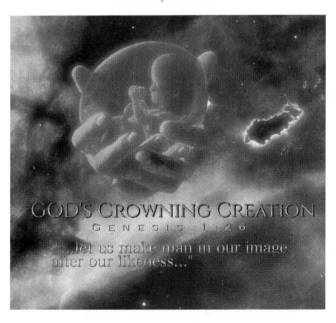

April 17

"The Lord works righteousness and justice for all who are oppressed. 7 He made known his ways to Moses, his acts to the people of Israel. 8 The Lord is merciful and gracious, slow to anger and abounding in steadfast love. 9 He will not always chide, nor will he keep his anger forever. 10 He does not deal with us according to our sins, nor repay us according to our iniquities."
(Psalms 103:6-10)

Lord Jesus, we ask that Your people will enter into 24/7, day and night unceasing prayer to end the oppression of abortion and senseless killing of the tiniest of our neighbors. Hear the cry of Your church as we pray for the harvest of those coming to abortion centers to 'get rid of the problem.' May we be found faithful in the house of the wise and the watchful to pray for deliverance and healing. Deliver us from thinking that someone else will always stand in the gap. In Jesus' Name, Amen!

April 18

"Now Cain talked with Abel his brother; and it came to pass, when they were in the field, that Cain rose up against Abel his brother and killed him. Then the Lord said to Cain, 'Where is Abel your brother?" He said, "I do not know. Am I my brother's keeper?'"
(Genesis 4:8-9

Father, help us to embrace the fact that we are our "brother's keeper." When, due to selfish motives, we try to cast off this responsibility please call us to account. Grant that we would be pleasing to you and to our "brothers," even the smallest in the womb. In Jesus' Name, Amen!

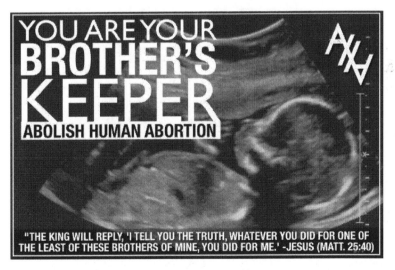

April 19

"And I say also unto thee, That thou art Peter, and upon this rock I will build my church; and the gates of hell shall not prevail against it. And I will give unto thee the keys of the kingdom of heaven: and whatsoever thou shalt bind on earth shall be bound in heaven: and whatsoever thou shalt loose on earth shall be loosed in heaven." (Matt 16:18-19)

Father, we are blessed with the gift of revelation of You and of the authority to bind and loose on this earth knowing that it is already bound or loosed in heaven. Thank You Lord. We bind the spirit of death and loose life on the corner of State and Slaughter St., Bristol, TN and any other place dedicated to the murdering of babies in the womb. Thank You that these gates of Hell will not prevail against Your church. We pray and agree with Your Word to choose life. In Jesus' Name, Amen!

April 20

"The thief comes only in order to steal and kill and destroy. I came that they may have and enjoy life, and have it in abundance (to the full, till it overflows)."
(John 10:10 AMP)

Dear Lord, the author and the giver of life; you make it clear that death and destruction are of the enemy. The abundant life, which comes only from you, begins with life, which begins at the moment of conception. Grace your church with insight and courage so that we might be champions of life, in our prayers, in our actions, and in our appeals to the seat of temporal power; in Jesus' Name, Amen!

April 21

"Wash yourselves, make yourselves clean; Put away the evil of your doings from before My eyes. Cease to do evil, learn to do good; seek justice, rebuke the oppressor; defend the fatherless, plead for the widow."
(Isaiah 1:16-17)

O God, our heavenly Father, give us courage and wisdom as we seek to eradicate the evil of abortion in our society. Help us to realize that your divine Spirit alone can change hearts and minds so that all your human creatures may enjoy the fullness of life you intend for them, beginning at conception and on to natural death. In Jesus' Name, Amen!

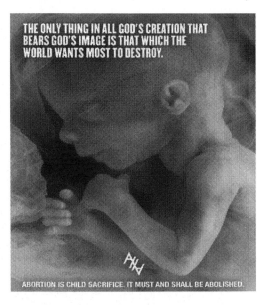

April 22

"Who is a God like You, pardoning iniquity and passing over the transgressions of the remnant of His heritage? He does not retain His anger forever, because He delights in mercy. He will again have compassion on us; and will subdue our iniquities."
(Micah 7:18-19)

Hear our prayer of repentance, Lord, and cleanse us from all unrighteousness. We praise you for your tender mercies and your compassion that never fails. Lord, it is only by Your grace that we can live lives that are just, and merciful. May Your Holy Spirit enable us to walk humbly in Your presence and may You be pleased to restore our nation so that a generation not yet born may praise you. In Jesus' Name, Amen!

April 23

"So you shall purge the guilt of innocent blood from your midst, when you do what is right in the sight of the LORD."
(Deuteronomy 21:9)

Father, how can we accomplish this other than by making it the law of the land that the rights of personhood under the 14th amendment begin at the moment of conception? May the church remain silent no more and speak with one voice to the seat of power - demanding life! In Jesus' Name, Amen!

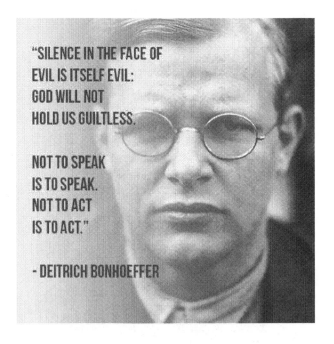

April 24

"Your eyes saw my substance, being yet unformed. And in Your book they all were written, the days fashioned for me, when as yet there were none of them."
(Psalm 139:16)

Gracious God, help us to appreciate the wonder and beauty of Your creation. Help us proclaim on behalf of every one of our fellow human beings, "I am fearfully and wonderfully made." May the knowledge that we are intimately known by You shape our lives and actions to bring about an end to legal abortion in our land. In Jesus' Name, Amen!

April 25

"How long, O Lord, will you look on? Rescue me from their destruction, my precious life from the lions!"

(Psalms 35:17)

O God, for almost half a century, the pre-born have been uttering this cry with their silent voices. Your church needs to speak up for them. Prepare us; send us; use us, all by the power of Your Spirit. Stir up more and more people everywhere to take up this great work, to bring an end to legalized abortion in America, and around the world. In Jesus' Name, Amen!

April 26

"When I consider Your heavens, the work of Your fingers, the moon and the stars, which You have ordained, what is man that You are mindful of him, and the son of man that You visit him? For You have made him a little lower than the angels, and You have crowned him with glory and honor."
(Psalm 8:3-5)

Lord, you are the creator of all things. Guide our thoughts to consider your creation in all of its majesty, beauty and holiness. Guide our hearts especially to your creation of precious human life, beginning at the moment of conception. Help us to comprehend how valuable all life is in your own heart, and embolden us to be champions for life. In Jesus' Name, Amen!

April 27

"In the beginning was the Word, and the Word was with God, and the Word was God. He was in the beginning with God. All things were made through Him, and without Him nothing was made that was made."
(John 1:1-3)

O God, may all people be quickened by Your Spirit to call you Father. And when we do, let your Spirit remind us that You love all people, from their beginning to their last day, and that all are given the opportunity to become your children. We praise you, Father, that you sent your Son, who through His death and resurrection, makes this possible. May we work and pray diligently to protect the sanctity of human life, that they all might come to know you through faith in Jesus Christ, in Whose Name we pray, Amen!

www.RememberingRoe.com

April 28

"Justice is turned back, And righteousness stands afar off; For truth is fallen in the street, And equity cannot enter."
(Isaiah 59:14)

Father, we pray repentance in our land and Your mercy over the pregnancy resource centers of the nation. We ask that free speech will be protected and that every pro-life center not be forced to post information about abortion centers. Father turn the battle at the gate of the Supreme Court and mark each member for the truth as defined in Your Court. Thank You in Jesus Name. Amen.

April 29

"I beseech you therefore brethren, by the mercies of God, that you present your bodies a living sacrifice, holy, acceptable to God, which is your reasonable service."
(Romans 12:1)

God Almighty, You alone are worthy of our praise and worship. Having accepted Your Son's sacrifice on our behalf, we in turn present our bodies to you as living sacrifices. We pray that you would use us as your vessels to rescue others who are perishing, even in the womb. In Jesus' Name, Amen!

April 30

"But the wisdom from above is first pure, then peaceable, gentle, open to reason, full of mercy and good fruits, impartial and sincere."
(James 3:17)

Father God, help your church to see that defending life in behalf of the unborn meets this definition of wisdom from above. Having seen this, then empower her to speak the truth to those still in darkness – from the streets to the seats of power.
In Jesus' Name, Amen!

May 1

You have heard it was said, 'you shall love your neighbor, and hate your enemy.' But I say to you, love your enemies, bless those who "curse you, do good to those who hate you, and pray for those who spitefully use you and persecute you."
(Matt 5: 43-44)

Heavenly Father, may we reflect your character of grace and kindness to those who hate us and curse us. Guard our hearts and our tongues as we respond in love to words and actions meant to rile us or cause us harm. Let others see the Hope that is Christ in all we say and do, and in the process, may all who are involved in the murder of babies be convicted to repent. In Jesus' Name, Amen.

May 2

*"In this you greatly rejoice, though now for a little
while, if need be, you have been grieved by various
trials, that the genuineness of your faith, being
much more precious than gold that perishes,
though it is tested by fire, may be found to praise,
honor and glory at the revelation of Jesus Christ."*
(1 Peter 1:6-7)

Dear Heavenly Father, there are times when we are
tempted to give up the fight for life. Help us to rise
up with wings of eagles as we press forward. Grant
us perseverance as you did your servant William
Wilberforce centuries ago. May we never grow
weary in well doing, knowing that in due season
we shall reap. In Jesus' Name, Amen!

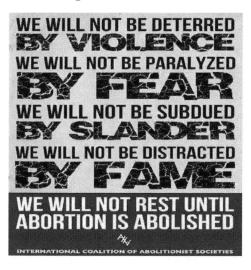

May 3

*"He will wipe every tear from their eyes. There
will be no more death or mourning or crying or
pain, for the old order of things has passed away.
He who was seated on the throne said, 'I am
making everything new!'"*
(Revelation 21:4-5)

Father, you are the God of hope. Your word fills us
with the vision of the world to come, when every
tear will be wiped away, and death will be no
more. Father, how we need the hope and strength
that comes from that vision! Keep our hearts
focused on heaven and diligent in the labors of
earth. As we struggle against the culture of death,
root our souls in the assurance of victory. In Jesus'
Name, Amen!

May 4

"...then the LORD God formed the man of dust from the ground and breathed into his nostrils the breath of life, and the man became a living creature."
(Genesis 2:7)

Father God, You are the author and the giver of life. In your Son there is life, and that life is the light of men. May the light of Christ so shine through us that the darkness of the culture of death, which has been normalized in our land, might be overcome. In Jesus' Name. Amen!

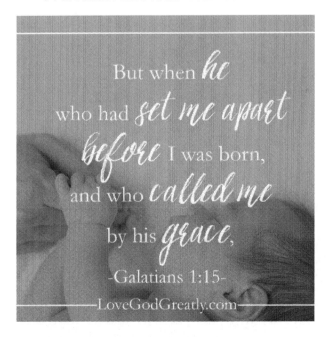

But when *he* who had *set me apart before* I was born, and who *called me* by his *grace,*
-Galatians 1:15-
LoveGodGreatly.com

May 5

"And for your lifeblood I will require a reckoning: from every beast I will require it and from man. From his fellow man I will require a reckoning for the life of man."
(Genesis 9:5)

Lord God, You are the author and creator of life. As such, every life is important to you. You require a reckoning for every life that is taken. Forgive us Lord for being complicit (actively or passively) in the taking of innocent lives in the womb. By your grace turn us into bold champions for life, in Jesus' Name, Amen!

May 6

"But if there is harm, then you shall pay life for life,"
(Exodus 21:23)

Almighty God, sometimes it takes the reading of only a few of your words to see the value you place on human life. It is terrifying to think of 61 million lives being required as payment for the 61 million babies that have been murdered in the womb. And that's just in the United States since abortion has been "legal." Oh Father, forgive us and strengthen us with a resolve to rid our nation of this abomination, in Jesus' Name, Amen!

May 7

"You shall not go around as a slanderer among your people, and you shall not stand up against the life of your neighbor: I am the LORD."
(Leviticus 19:16.)

Lord God, even the most vulnerable among us is our neighbor. We must speak for those who cannot speak, and defend the weak. We should stand against the death of our neighbor. Motivate and empower us to do just that, in Jesus' Name, Amen!

This is what we all looked like at 12 weeks in the womb. Legal to kill in all 50 states. Anyone think its not a person? Pass this along. It literally might save a life.

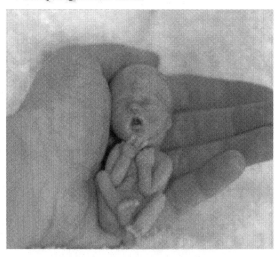

May 8

"Whoever takes a human life shall surely be put to death."
Leviticus 24:17

O God, what can we say? Your attitude towards the taking of innocent human life is clear. That is why we are grateful for the shed blood of Jesus, and that His resurrection validates the fact that it is the full and acceptable payment for our sins. From the strength of your forgiveness, may we become the champions of life, just as you are. In Jesus' Name, Amen!

May 9

*"See, I have set before you today life and good,
death and evil. - I call heaven and earth to witness
against you today, that I have set before you life
and death, blessing and curse. Therefore choose
life, that you and your offspring may live,"*
(Deuteronomy 30:15,19)

Dear Lord, You gave us the right and the
responsibility of choice. May we always choose
life, by our prayers, our thoughts, and our deeds.
Life is good; death is evil. Continue to expose the
dark evil of abortion, and rouse the church from
her apathy, until righteousness is once again
restored to our land. In Jesus' Name, Amen!

May 10

"And Manoah said, 'Now when your words come true, what is to be the child's manner of life, and what is his mission?'"
(Judges 13:12)

Father God, it is clear from Your word that You have a plan and a purpose for every person. May every Father and Mother have their hearts turned towards their children to give them every chance of achieving that plan and purpose. May our prayers and efforts be effective in changing the laws of the land so that they bestow personhood status on people from the moment of conception until natural death. In Jesus' Name, Amen!

May 11

"Behold, as your life was precious this day in my sight, so may my life be precious in the sight of the LORD, and may he deliver me out of all tribulation."
(1 Samuel 26:24)

O God, Creator and sustainer of all life, and the ultimate authority to declare that life is precious - work in us to will and to do of your good pleasure; to bring an end to legalized abortion in the USA, and even the world. In Jesus' Name, Amen!

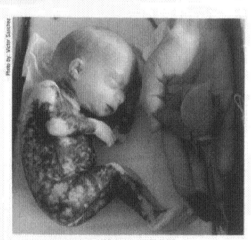

A BABY DIED

This is Baby Choice, a precious 4½ month old little girl, burned by the saline solution used to abort her. There are 4000 babies aborted each day in America, (one every 20 seconds). Abortion is legal thru the ninth month of pregnancy.
We have been led to believe that having an abortion is removing a mass of tissue. LOOK AT THIS LITTLE GIRL; she is more than a mass of tissue. She is a perfectly formed human being! IS THIS SUCH A GOOD CHOICE?

© 1989 Debbie Hudnall, Victory For The Unborn, P.O. Box 690762, Houston, TX 77269-0762
(713) 890-1321

May 12

"Then he stretched himself upon the child three times and cried to the LORD, "O LORD my God, let this child's life come into him again." And the LORD listened to the voice of Elijah. And the life of the child came into him again, and he revived."
(1Kings 17:21-22)

Creator God, author and sustainer of life - we see that life is so important to you that on occasion you intervene in the natural order of events and cause life to triumph over death. May we, as your children, be similar champions for life. Lord, restore righteousness to the land and end abortion. In Jesus' Name, Amen!

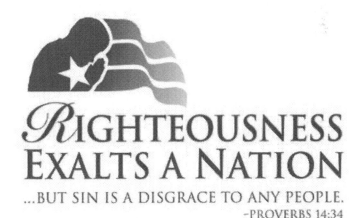

RIGHTEOUSNESS
EXALTS A NATION
...BUT SIN IS A DISGRACE TO ANY PEOPLE.
-PROVERBS 14:34

May 13

*"You have granted me life and steadfast love, and
your care has preserved my spirit."*
(Job 10:12)

Our God and Father, You are the One who grants
life, and Who preserves the spirit. Forgive us for
deeming one life more valuable than another. May
the practice of child sacrifice at the altar of
convenience come to an end really soon. In Jesus'
Name, Amen!

May 14

"In his hand is the life of every living thing and the breath of all mankind."
(Job 12:10)

Heavenly Father - forgive us for playing God. Forgive our nation for playing God. Forgive the church for not properly representing God. Change our hearts, one and all, to cherish human life at all stages and in all forms, and to leave the beginning, the middle, and the end in your very capable hands. In Jesus' Name, Amen!

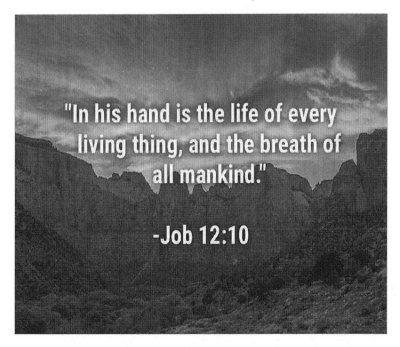

May 15

*"Give justice to the weak and the fatherless;
maintain the right of the afflicted and the destitute.
Rescue the weak and the needy; deliver them from
the hand of the wicked."*
(Psalm 82:3-4 ESV)

Lord God Almighty, help us to realize that we,
your people, are called to impart justice, to rescue
the weak and needy. We are not called to just sit
back and expect You to act. Often your actions are
a response to our actions (or inaction). May we be
motivated to take up your cause in the power of the
Holy Spirit, in the Name of Jesus, Amen!

May 16

"The Spirit of God has made me, and the breath of the Almighty gives me life."
(Job 33:4)

Lord God, Creator of heaven and earth and all that dwell therein, life is and should be in your hands. Forgive us as individuals, as a church, and as a nation, for taking that prerogative from You. We do this either by evil actions, or apathetic inaction. Forgive us, we pray, and empower us to take good and positive action to rid our land of the evil genocide. In Jesus' Name, Amen!

May 17

"My times are in your hand; rescue me from the hand of my enemies and from my persecutors!"
(Psalm 31:15)

Heavenly Father, as we pray this Scripture, we think not only of the 100's and 1000's afflicted by the atrocities of the Syrian war, but of the 1,000,000's whose lives are taken as they are ripped from the womb. May we be instruments of your justice and rescue. In Jesus' Name, Amen!

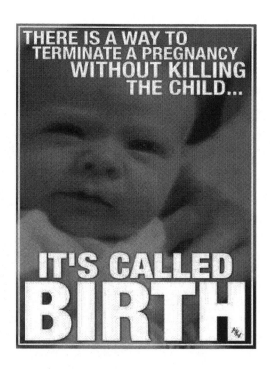

May 18

"...therefore I despise myself, and repent in dust and ashes."
(Job 42:6)

"If a man does not repent, God will whet his sword; he has bent and readied his bow;
(Psalm 7:12)

Gracious God, we pray today for a wholesale repentance on the part of your church and of our nation concerning the issue of abortion. We thank you that during 40 Days for Life campaigns a number of abortion workers have had actual conversion experiences and left their jobs. May that happen on such a grand scale that abortion vanishes from the land. In Jesus' Name, Amen!

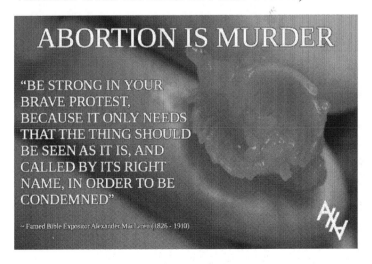

May 19

"So you shall remember and do all my commandments, and be holy to your God."
(Numbers 15:40)

Lord God, there is a day on the calendar marked "Holocaust Remembrance Day." Replacement Theology on the part of the church aided and abetted that tragedy. That wrong theology continues today, even while we cry "Never again!" Yet 46 plus years ago another holocaust began and continues today. Anthropocentric Theology continues to aid and abet, so that the death toll is 10 times higher. Give us grace to repent and to set a new course, in Jesus' Name, Amen!

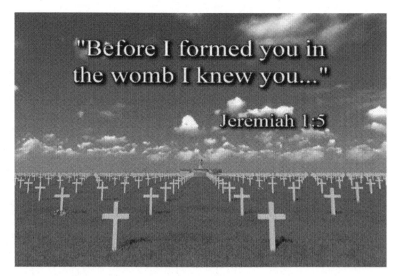

May 20

" 'Were they ashamed when they committed abomination? No, they were not at all ashamed; they did not know how to blush. Therefore they shall fall among those who fall; at the time that I punish them, they shall be overthrown,' says the Lord."
(Jeremiah 6:15)

Heavenly Father, there are those in this world who practice the abomination of abortion, and there are those who celebrate the deed as though it were some sort of divine blessing. Lord, deliver those bound in such darkness; remove the blinders that keep them from seeing. Use us as you see fit in that endeavor, in Jesus' Name, Amen!

SHOUTYOURABORTION.COM
Shout Your Abortion — I am 23 and I have had 3 abortions. YES I HAVE!

May 21

"Do not sweep my soul away with sinners, nor my life with bloodthirsty men,"
(Psalm 26:9)

Lord, that Psalm is our prayer. Your church has idly stood by as innocent little ones are being led to the slaughter of abortion. That places us placidly in agreement with bloodthirsty men. You seem to be waiting for your church to rise up and say, "ENOUGH!" Enough, in Jesus' Name, Amen!

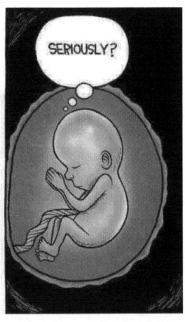

May 22

"For I hear the whispering of many-- terror on every side!-- as they scheme together against me, as they plot to take my life."
(Psalm 31:13)

Father God, in the abortuaries across America, some 3,000 babies, if they could speak, would be saying this Psalm. May we be their voice, and may we be your voice as you empower us to speak effectively to the seats of power, "End Abortion." We purport to be a government of the people, so let the people speak. In Jesus' Name, Amen!

May 23

"Let them be put to shame and dishonor who seek after my life! Let them be turned back and disappointed who devise evil against me!"
(Psalm 35:4)

Lord God, in behalf of the babies being led to slaughter today, we cry out Psalm 35:4. To that we add - may those brought to shame and dishonor repent of their evil ways and turn to you. May those who once chose death, now choose life that they and their offspring might live. In Jesus' Name, Amen!

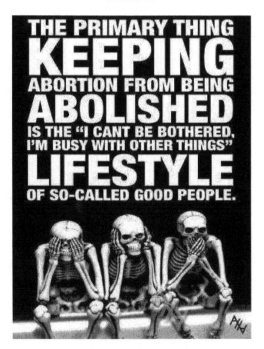

May 24

*"For without cause they hid their net for me;
without cause they dug a pit for my life."*
(Psalm 35:7)

Father God - as we look through your word,
procreation (the birthing of human offspring) is the
natural order of things and was so from the
beginning. Forgive us for taking it into our own
hands to interrupt that order with the abomination
of abortion, and for then making it the de facto law
of the land. Forgive we the people and we the
church for allowing this to happen with barely a
whimper of protest. May the Lion of the tribe of
Judah well up big within us and roar: "NO
MORE!"In Jesus' Name, Amen!

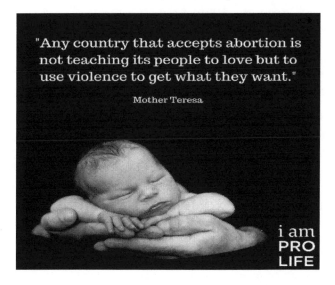

"Any country that accepts abortion is
not teaching its people to love but to
use violence to get what they want."

Mother Teresa

i am
PRO
LIFE

May 25

"How long, O Lord, will you look on? Rescue me from their destruction, my precious life from the lions!"
(Psalm 35:17

It is only because of your mercies O Lord that we are not all consumed. The lions referenced above could well include all trapped in the deception of abortion rights. May your goodness and mercy lead many to repentance - turning from death to life; turning from apathy to action - that abortion will come to an end. In Jesus' Name, Amen!

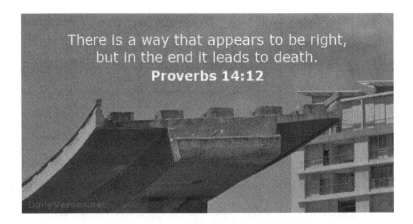

There is a way that appears to be right, but in the end it leads to death.
Proverbs 14:12

May 26

"Those who seek my life lay their snares; those who seek my hurt speak of ruin and meditate treachery all day long."
(Psalm 38:12)

Lord God Almighty, ruin and treachery, profit and greed, comfort and convenience are all entwined in the sin of abortion. If it were just murder, many would wash their hands and say it doesn't involve them. But it involves us all. May we all speak with one voice to the seats of power demanding that the righteous foundation of life be restored to our land.
In Jesus' Name, Amen.

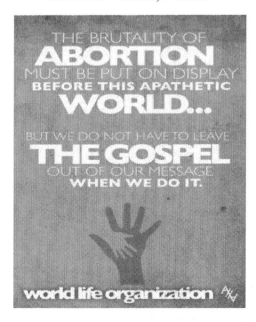

May 27

"When Mordecai learned all that had been done, Mordecai tore his clothes and put on sackcloth and ashes, and went out into the midst of the city, and he cried out with a loud and bitter cry."
(Esther 4:1 ESV)

Father God, when RedState contributor Kira Davis, encourages parents to do all they can to stop the implementation of a new California Sex Education Law she says "Make noise. Lots and lots and lots of noise…When constituents get cranky, lawmakers pay attention…and so few people actually call and write anymore that just a few hundred voices go a very long way..." So may your church speak with ONE LOUD VOICE in defense of life. In Jesus' Name, Amen!

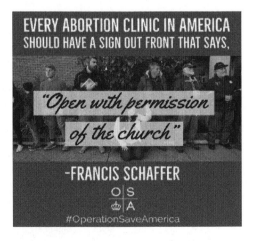

May 28

"Let those be put to shame and disappointed altogether who seek to snatch away my life; let those be turned back and brought to dishonor who delight in my hurt!"
(Psalm 40:14)

Lord God, turn back Planned Parenthood; bring total dishonor upon them and their bloody agenda. Shut them down we pray. May the people's hearts turn to life, and may our government once again honor life as an inalienable right which comes from you. In Jesus' Name, Amen!

May 29

"For strangers have risen against me; ruthless men seek my life; they do not set God before themselves. Selah"
(Psalm 54:3)

Father God, as we pause and think about that verse, we realize that the people who wield the instruments of death against innocent little ones in the womb are complete strangers to their victims. Money and convenience are all gods who have replaced you. Deception and confusion all play their part. Use us, our prayers, and our actions, to bring about an end to the vicious cycle, in Jesus' Name, Amen!

Support the Assault Weapons BAN!

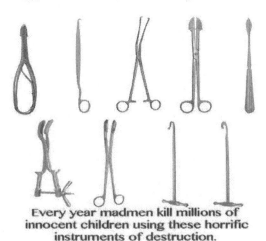

Every year madmen kill millions of innocent children using these horrific instruments of destruction.

May 30

"In him was life, and the life was the light of men."
(John 1:4)

Father God, how far we have fallen as a nation when we consider the very beginnings of human life as no life at all. At least we, who claim to follow Christ, should embrace the life which He is and which He imparts. Stir us up O God to stand up for life and to defend the defenseless. Help us to make the end of abortion in our land a true Memorial Day, in Jesus' Name, Amen!

May 31

*"Greater love has no one than this, that someone
lay down his life for his friends."*
(John 15:13)

Almighty God, on this day when we pause and
remember those who have risked laying down their
lives for others in some distant land, we also think
of the One who laid down His life on the cross.
Neither one died so that we could murder babies. It
was for freedom's sake that Christ has set us free,
yet we seem to have become ensnared again in
yokes of bondage. Provoke us, as a church and as a
nation, to be willing to lay down our lives, as it
were, in behalf of the innocent little people in the
womb, in Jesus' Name, Amen!

June 1

"For my enemies speak concerning me; those who watch for my life consult together"
(Psalm 71:10)

Heavenly Father, in 1973 various forces came together to consult on the matter of life. Leaving you out of the discussion, they relied on wisdom from the world system controlled by Satan. Those who looked to your Word for information as to when human life begins knew that it begins at conception. Science has since gone on to prove that very fact, yet we remain in a culture of death. Everywhere we look we see blood begetting blood. Free us O God from our willful ignorance and grant us the grace to embrace life, from conception until natural end. In Jesus' Name, Amen!

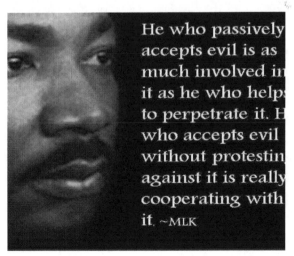

He who passively accepts evil is as much involved in it as he who helps to perpetrate it. He who accepts evil without protesting against it is really cooperating with it. ~MLK

June 2

Christ prayed, *"not that you should take them out of the world, but that you should keep them from the evil. They are not of the world, even as I am not of the world."*
(John 17:15-16)

For many, free will is dangerously overriding God's perfect will. Evidence of this is that the latest Barna Survey revealed 27% of born again Christians said abortion was not a moral issue. Dear Lord, help us to embrace and stand up for your perfect will. Your will is life, and that more abundantly. Revive us again that we might defend the inalienable right of life, given to us by You. In Jesus' Name, Amen!

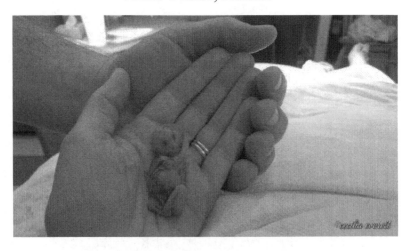

12 week old miscarried baby.

June 3

"They band together against the life of the righteous and condemn the innocent to death."
(Psalm 94:21)

Our God and Father, although every child is conceived in iniquity, they are innocent of personal sin. Save them from death in the womb, that they might grow and be given an opportunity to know you as Savior and Lord. May we help them and all who might consider doing them harm by proclaiming your Name in all we say and do.
Amen!

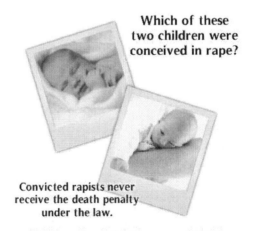

Which of these two children were conceived in rape?

Convicted rapists never receive the death penalty under the law.

Neither should the innocent child.

100% PRO-LIFE   Abortion always kills an innocent human being.

www.facebook.com/avoiceforhope

June 4

"In your steadfast love give me life, that I may keep the testimonies of your mouth."
(Psalm 119:88)

Lord God Almighty, we pray for all the innocent little ones, especially for those in the womb. May every parent and every governmental authority be aligned with You and Your precepts. May we open our mouths in this righteous cause that these little ones would be allowed to experience life, where they grow to declare Your majesty with their own mouths. In Jesus' Name, Amen!

"Do not murder a child by abortion or kill a newborn infant."

Taken from The Didache: The Teaching of the 12 Apostles First Century AD

June 5

"Hear my voice according to your steadfast love;
O LORD, according to your justice give me life."
(Psalm 119:149)

Father God, we plead this as a prayer in behalf of those who have no voice - the babies in the womb and the Alfie Evans' of the world. Bring down the unjust system of man, inspired by the father of lies, and replace it with a just system based on the truth. In the Name of Jesus, Who is The Truth, we pray, Amen!

June 6

"Such are the ways of everyone who is greedy for unjust gain; it takes away the life of its possessors."
(Proverbs 1:19)

Almighty God, while greed is not the only motive behind the murder of babies in the womb, it certainly plays a big part. Today we pray that You would turn to You the hearts of those whose greed leads to this abomination or turn them out of their bloody occupation. In Jesus' Name, Amen!

"As an abortionist, I see how abortion affects everyone connected with the child who dies. I REGRET performing abortions."
Dr. Anthony Levantino

AbortionShockwaves.com/August

June 7

"...be attentive to my words; incline your ear to my sayings. Let them not escape from your sight; keep them within your heart. For they are life to those who find them, and healing to all their flesh."
(Proverbs 4:20-22)

Lord God Almighty, Creator and Sustainer of all life, we beseech you today to open the eyes of many who have been deceived by the culture of death. We recognize that Satan is the deceiver, and he is a murderer. Grant us grace to see what is going on and to attack it in the power of the Holy Spirit, in Jesus' Name, Amen!

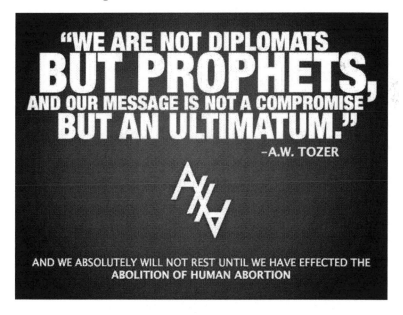

June 8

*"The wage of the righteous leads to life, the gain
of the wicked to sin."*
(Proverbs 10:16)

Almighty God, we agree with you that there is
none righteous, no not one. How amazing is your
grace that you would redeem the likes of me and
impute the righteousness of Jesus to me and then
empower me by your Spirit to become righteous. If
you can do it for and to me, you can do it for and
to anybody. Turn the hearts of the wicked away
from genocide (in thought, word, deed, and law)
and turn them to life, in Jesus' Name, Amen!

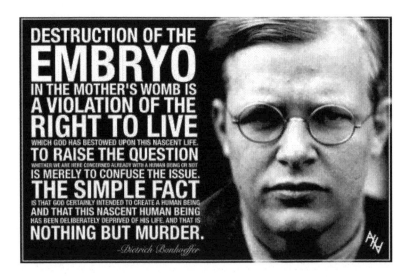

June 9

"The fear of the LORD prolongs life, but the years of the wicked will be short."
(Proverbs 10:27)

Lord God, may this nation, may your church, may our government all come under the fear of the Lord, that life may be prolonged. Life is both a gift from You, and an unalienable right from you. May we begin to see life through your eyes and then reflect what we see in all we do. In Jesus' Name, Amen!

The Church only faintly and infrequently condemns abortion. The result is that though it says, "abortion is wrong", what everyone hears is, "but not all THAT wrong".

June 10

"In the path of righteousness is life, and in its pathway there is no death."
(Proverbs 12:28)

Lord God Almighty, have mercy on us. As a nation we have adopted a culture of death in which there is no righteousness. As your people we have become complacent, and if we haven't adopted this culture, we have aided and abetted it by our silence. May your church repent and rise up with one voice proclaiming, "Yes to Life" and "No to Death!" In Jesus' Name, Amen!

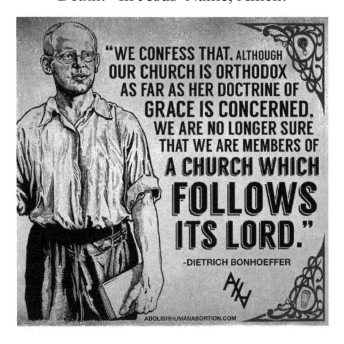

June 11

*"The fear of the LORD is a fountain of life, that
one may turn away from the snares of death."*
(Proverbs 14:27)

God, our El-Shaddai, may we fear you once again,
as individuals, as your church, and as a nation -
that we might enjoy a fountain of life, turning from
the snares of death that have taken us captive.
Show us our complicity, that we may find grace to
repent. In Jesus' Name, Amen!

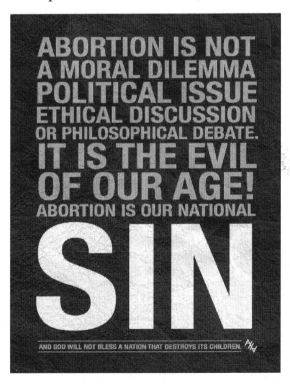

June 12

*"The ear that listens to life-giving reproof will
dwell among the wise."*
(Proverbs 15:31)

Heavenly Father, may your church have ears to
hear Your reproof, and then give us the boldness to
declare life-giving reproof to all of those engaged
in the culture of death. Even we, your people, are
guilty of participation because of our silence. By
your grace, may we apply our hearts unto wisdom
to bring an end to legalized abortion. In Jesus'
Name, Amen!

*"The silent and dormant
church is the abortion
industry's biggest ally. The
abortion holocaust would end
overnight if just a fraction of
the nation's 500,000
churches became active in
the fight."
- Mark Crutcher, Life
Dynamics*

June 13

"Good sense is a fountain of life to him who has it,
but the instruction of fools is folly."
(Proverbs 16:22)

Father God, thank you for revealing to us that
which makes sense. It is revealed in your creation
of the natural world and it is revealed in your
Word. Open the eyes of our understanding that the
obvious good sense of human life beginning at
conception would become the law of the land. In
Jesus' Name, Amen!

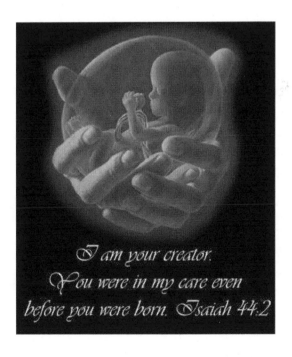

I am your creator.
You were in my care even
before you were born. Isaiah 44:2

June 14

"The fear of the LORD leads to life, and whoever has it rests satisfied; he will not be visited by harm."
(Proverbs 19:23)

Almighty God, in reverent fear we bow before you, while coming boldly to your throne of grace, to obtain mercy and grace to help in time of need. We need you like never before. We ask that the heart of this nation be turned to you. Draw even those who have participated in the 60+ million abortions over the past 46 years to repentance. May our fear lead to life, that we might escape judgment. In Jesus' Name, Amen!

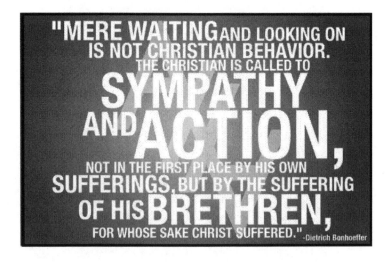

June 15

"...for the LORD will plead their cause and rob of life those who rob them."
(Proverbs 22:23)

Lord God, You are the Creator and giver of life. All life flows from you. Satan, on the other hand, is a murderer from the beginning. Death will one day be swallowed up in victory, and those who rob the innocent of life will they themselves be robbed. Grant us repentance before that great and terrible Day, that our hearts and our laws would affirm life, from the moment of conception, in Jesus' Name, Amen!

June 16

"Bloodthirsty men hate one who is blameless and seek the life of the upright."
(Proverbs 29:10)

Lord God Almighty, although every one of us has been conceived in iniquity, there are none more upright in their natural state than innocent children, especially those in the womb. We cry out for an ending of the bloodshed. Restore righteousness to the land. Grant us repentance, in Jesus' Name, Amen!

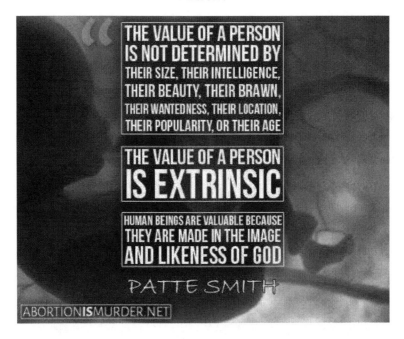

June 17

"Though a sinner does evil a hundred times and prolongs his life, yet I know that it will be well with those who fear God, because they fear before him."
(Ecclesiastes 8:12)

Eternal God, this Scripture causes us to pause and ask You to give us, and all men, an eternal perspective. Evil acts spring from evil hearts, calloused over so that the eternity you placed there is not functioning. Awaken eternity in us that we all might choose life. In Jesus' Name, Amen!

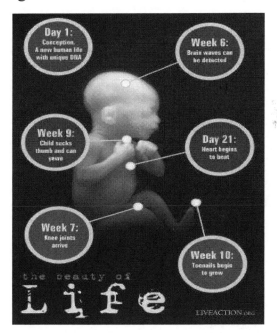

June 18

"And to this people you shall say: 'Thus says the LORD: Behold, I set before you the way of life and the way of death.'"
(Jeremiah 21:8)

Lord, it has been this way since you created men in your image. We can choose life or death. Help us to choose life. The Supreme Court opened the gates of hell and death when they professed to not know when life begins. All we have to do is consult your Word to know that life begins at conception. May our thoughts, actions, and laws reflect this truth. In Jesus Name, Amen!

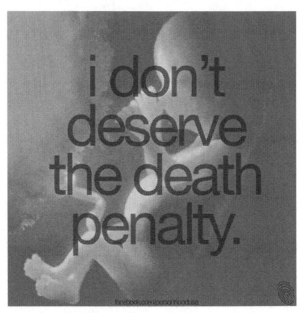

June 19

"Sing to the LORD; praise the LORD! For he has delivered the life of the needy from the hand of evildoers."
(Jeremiah 20:13)

Heavenly Father, may we even now, sing to You and praise You for the promised delivery of the needy from the hands of evil people who seek to do them harm. Those in the womb are the neediest of them all. May we as a people cooperate with your deliverance by proclaiming life, and enacting laws protecting life from the moment of conception, lest we be caught up in your judgment. In Jesus' Name, Amen!

June 20

"Posterity shall serve him; it shall be told of the Lord to the coming generation;"
(Psalms 22:30)

Lord, Your intention is that your greatness and goodness be told, from generation to generation, Because you are the giver and sustainer of life, may we always choose, and champion for life wherever it is denied. May legalized baby murder come to an end, that many generations would live and come to know You. In Jesus 'Name, Amen!

When You Abort a Baby
You Don't Just Abort One Person
...You Abort Generations

Defend Preborn Babies

June 21

There was a feeling among the Jewish people during the years of the great holocaust that every mass celebrated and every sermon preached that did not mention the genocide was a silent approval of same.

YHWH Elohim, God of Abraham, Isaac, and Jacob, is it possible that the Jewish view of the church's complicity in the holocaust was accurate? Is it possible that the church is complicit once again in giving silent approval to the genocide that has been happening in this country for more than 46 years? It would seem so. Oh God have mercy on us and awaken us from our apathy. May our repentance be accompanied by visible fruit - an end to legalized abortion, in Jesus' Name, Amen!

June 22

"If I say to the wicked, 'You shall surely die,' and you give him no warning, nor speak to warn the wicked from his wicked way, in order to save his life, that wicked person shall die for his iniquity, but his blood I will require at your hand."
(Ezekiel 3:18)

And so Lord God Almighty, let it be declared that all those who participate, actively and passively in the abomination of genocide do wickedly. You say, "Repent, lest you die because of your iniquity." Lord, raise up every member of your body to sound the clarion call - "No more legalized abortion in the land." In Jesus' Name, Amen!

June 23

"Also on your skirts is found the blood of the souls of the poor innocents: I have not found it by secret search, but plainly upon all these things."
(Jeremiah 2:34)

Lord God, we as a nation have not only legalized abominable acts, but we have funded them and paraded them around, calling them good rather than evil. Your church has been complicit in this by its silence. Forgive us Lord, and grant us grace to be salt and light once again. As we fight the good fight of faith, may that include the fight for life. In Jesus' Name, Amen!

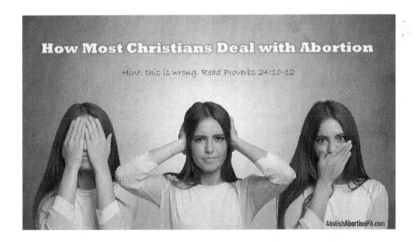

June 24

"Rescue those who are being taken away to death;
hold back those who are stumbling to the
slaughter."
(Proverbs 24:11)

Father, may we, like the Bulgarian Orthodox
Church and the Confessing Church of northern
Germany, who stepped in between the Jews and
the Nazi powers who would take them away to
death, step in between the precious little ones in
the womb and the powers that would lead them to
slaughter. May we intervene by our prayers, our
presence, and our petitions to power, in Jesus
Name, Amen!

June 25

"Again, when a wicked person turns away from the wickedness he has committed and does what is just and right, he shall save his life. "
(Ezekiel 18:27)

Lord God, we agree with You and Your Word that abortion is murder and that murder is a violation of your commandment. Yet in your mercy you allow every sinner, even the murderer, the opportunity to repent. You even give us the grace to repent and to walk in righteousness. May repentance bring about a restoration of righteous foundations to our nation, our churches, and our personal lives; in Jesus Name, Amen!

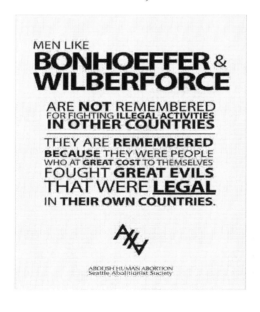

MEN LIKE
BONHOEFFER &
WILBERFORCE
ARE **NOT** REMEMBERED
FOR FIGHTING **ILLEGAL ACTIVITIES**
IN OTHER COUNTRIES
THEY ARE **REMEMBERED**
BECAUSE THEY WERE PEOPLE
WHO AT **GREAT COST** TO THEMSELVES
FOUGHT GREAT EVILS
THAT WERE **LEGAL**
IN **THEIR OWN COUNTRIES.**

ABOLISH HUMAN ABORTION
Seattle Abolitionist Society

June 26

"You have devised shame for your house by cutting off many peoples; you have forfeited your life."
(Habakkuk 2:10)

Almighty God, from our perspective it seems as though You are slow to anger and slow to judge. We get impatient when it is someone else who benefits from that, often forgetting that it is for the very same reason that we have not perished. When you do judge, it is in righteousness and holy wrath. The house of America, and that of many other nations, is guilty of cutting off life through the genocide of abortion. There will be a reckoning at some time - blood for blood. May we wake up and repent. May the lament of your church rise to a deafening roar, in Jesus' Name, Amen!

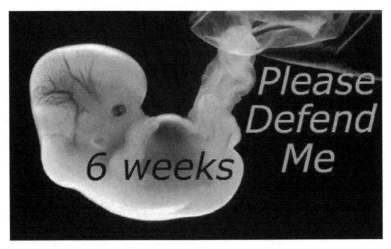

June 27

*"And these will go away into eternal punishment,
but the righteous into eternal life."*
(Matthew 25:46)

Lord God, by your grace, enable us to be on the right side of this equation. May our prayers, our petitions, and our positions concerning "the least of these" always be in support of life. May we preach eternal life in Jesus alone, while standing for all human life, from its unique beginning. In Jesus' Name, Amen!

June 28

"For whoever would save his life will lose it, but whoever loses his life for my sake and the gospel's will save it."
(Mark 8:35)

Father, forgive us for those times when we have been unwilling to lose our lives for your sake and for the gospel's. Forgive us for our spiritualized rationalizations where we separate the preaching of the gospel from the call to be salt and light. Forgive us for turning blind eyes to evil and calling it love. Help us to crucify the flesh and be willing to lose our lives in the battle for life, in Jesus' Name, Amen!

June 29

"Reuben, you are my firstborn, My might and the beginning of my strength, The excellency of dignity and the excellency of power."
(Genesis 49:3 NKJV)

Jehovah God, please don't let small steps in the right direction obscure the goal of personhood for everyone, beginning at the moment of conception. Help us to see clearly that abortion is not health care in need of regulation, but genocide in need of abolition. In Jesus' Name, Amen!

June 30

"And he said to all, 'If anyone would come after me, let him deny himself and take up his cross daily and follow me.'"
(Luke 9:23)

Almighty God, there are some 80,000,000 Evangelicals in the USA. Many are hearing about their destiny, their purpose, the power within them, etc. Yet most will spend another week never seeing their purpose as defending life; never using their power to preach the gospel at an abortion mill or to call their congressman demanding passage of a Personhood Bill. God forgive us for making the gospel so much about "me" and so little about You and them. In Jesus' Name, Amen!

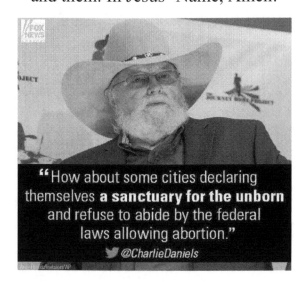

"How about some cities declaring themselves **a sanctuary for the unborn** and refuse to abide by the federal laws allowing abortion."
@CharlieDaniels

PRAY FOR THE UNBORN: The Power of Fervent Prayer

Pray for the unborn
Those with no voice (Proverbs 31:8-9)
They lay at the mercy
Of those who preach choice
The killing of children
It never ceases
The precious unborn
They're beaten to pieces (Isaiah 3:15)
Pray for the unborn
Unable to speak ((Proverbs 31:8-9)
We who are strong
Must speak for the weak (Romans 15:1)
Pray for the unborn
(They're) delivered to slaughter (Romans 24:11-12)
By those who despise
Their own sons and daughters
Pray for the unborn
If for no others
Delivered to death
By their fathers and mothers
In this heartless world
Where very few care
They need our actions
Our thoughts words and prayers (Luke 18:1)
So pray for the unborn
Pray for God's touch
The prayers of the righteous
Accomplishes much (James 5:16)

Linen, M. (2018). Death Roe: State Funded Racism, Torture, and Murder. Unpublished manuscript

July 1

"My covenant with him [Levi] was one of life and peace, and I gave them to him. It was a covenant of fear, and he feared me. He stood in awe of my name. But you have turned aside from the way. You have caused many to stumble by your instruction. You have corrupted the covenant of Levi, says the Lord of hosts,."
(Malachi 2:5, 8)

Lord God Almighty, we, like the priests of Malachi's time have profaned Your Name by giving outright or tacit approval to those things which You detest. We have allowed the sanctity of life and of marriage to be violated by unrighteous judgments and laws, uttering barely a whimper as we go about our lives. We have stood idly by as love has been redefined as tolerance. This is not how a holy priesthood should behave. Restore us, we pray, to our true calling. in Jesus' Name, Amen!

ABORTION
CANNOT BE MADE SAFE
IT ALWAYS ENDS IN SOMEONE DYING

WE WILL NOT REST
UNTIL WE HAVE EFFECTED IS ABOLITION

July 2

*"Whoever believes in the Son has eternal life;
whoever does not obey the Son shall not see life,
but the wrath of God remains on him."*
(John 3:36)

Merciful and gracious God, we deserve your wrath
because of our disobedience. Only by repenting
and coming to the cross can we obtain forgiveness.
We repent for our nation for legalizing the murder
of innocent babies in the womb. We repent of our
apathy which has pretty much allowed this to
happen for 46 years and counting. We cry out to
you, to each other, and to the seats of power:
"Abolish abortion, in Jesus' Name, Amen!"

*"...yet I am not silenced because of the darkness,
nor because thick darkness covers my face."*
(Job 23:17)

Father God, open our ears to the silent cries of the
unborn as they are being murdered in the womb.
As we hear them, open our mouths to speak in
their behalf. If not us, who? If not now, when?
How long can we mouth the words, "God bless
America" without also crying aloud, "Abolish
abortion"? In Jesus' Name, Amen!

July 4

"Greater love has no one than this, that someone lay down his life for his friends."
(John 15:13)

Lord God, how the mighty have fallen. We have gone from a nation whose heroes lay down their lives to save the lives of others to a nation that has legalized the murder of over 60 million babies in the past 46 years. O God, bring us back to our senses; shake us from our apathy. In Jesus' Name, Amen!

July 5

"Already the one who reaps is receiving wages and gathering fruit for eternal life, so that sower and reaper may rejoice together."
(John 4:36)

Heavenly Father, empower us to bring the gospel to the streets, to the killing places, and to the seats of power. Help us to sow life that life might be the fruit to be gathered, not just for babies, but for mothers, fathers, abortion workers, legislators, and judges. You have given us the words of life, now may we use them for your glory. In Jesus' Name, Amen!

I BELIEVE therefore I SPEAK.
2 Corinthians 4:13

July 6

"...and come out, those who have done good to the resurrection of life, and those who have done evil to the resurrection of judgment."
(John 5:29)

Lord God Almighty, for every promised blessing there seems to be a promised terror. Even when the "good news" is proclaimed, there is "bad news" for those who reject it. By either means may we persuade men to choose life and may our laws be such that they protect life - the first unalienable right. In Jesus' Name, Amen!

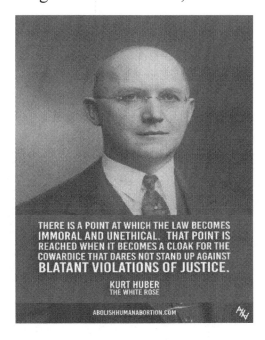

THERE IS A POINT AT WHICH THE LAW BECOMES IMMORAL AND UNETHICAL. THAT POINT IS REACHED WHEN IT BECOMES A CLOAK FOR THE COWARDICE THAT DARES NOT STAND UP AGAINST **BLATANT VIOLATIONS OF JUSTICE.**
KURT HUBER
THE WHITE ROSE

ABOLISHHUMANABORTION.COM

July 7

"In you, O LORD, do I take refuge; let me never be put to shame! In your righteousness deliver me and rescue me; incline your ear to me, and save me!"
(Psalm 71:1-2)

Father God, today we pray that you would speak to all those who are about to choose or facilitate death by abortion. May they hear You calling them to take refuge in You. If they hear your call after the fact, let them know that there is still refuge in You, for You desire to deliver and save us all, in and through Christ Jesus, Amen!

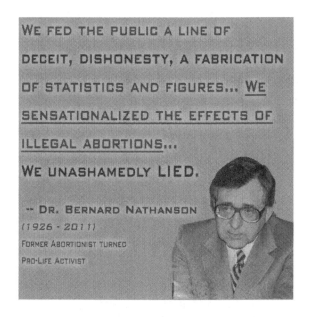

WE FED THE PUBLIC A LINE OF DECEIT, DISHONESTY, A FABRICATION OF STATISTICS AND FIGURES... WE SENSATIONALIZED THE EFFECTS OF ILLEGAL ABORTIONS...

WE UNASHAMEDLY LIED.

-- DR. BERNARD NATHANSON
(1926 - 2011)
FORMER ABORTIONIST TURNED
PRO-LIFE ACTIVIST

July 8

"...you refuse to come to me that you may have life."
(John 5:40)

Heavenly Father, how different it is for those who truly know You and love You. You are life; You are light - O pierce the darkness that blinds men's souls. May they know You that they might know life, and knowing life, let them choose life. In Jesus' Name, Amen!

July 9

"Jesus said to them, "I am the bread of life; whoever comes to me shall not hunger, and whoever believes in me shall never thirst."
(John 6:35)

Heavenly Father, You made us so that we all hunger for something that satisfies. Irresponsible sex doesn't satisfy; being free from the responsibilities of parenting doesn't satisfy; piles of money from ill-gotten gain don't satisfy. Only Jesus, the Bread of Life, satisfies. We pray that many will come to Him and will choose life. Until then, may our nation enact righteous laws clarifying that under the 14th amendment, personhood begins at the moment of conception. In Jesus' Name, Amen.

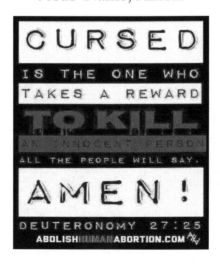

July 10

"It is the Spirit who gives life; the flesh is no help at all. The words that I have spoken to you are spirit and life."
(John 6:63)

Lord Almighty, Maker of heaven and earth - breath on us the breath of life. Give us a holy discontent with the works of the flesh. Fill us with your Spirit, with your Word, and with your passion - that we might be supernatural champions for life in the midst of a culture fixated on death. In Jesus' Name, Amen!

July 11

*"The thief comes only to steal and kill and destroy.
I came that they may have life and have it
abundantly."*
(John 10:10)

Father God, it is clear from this verse alone who is
behind the culture of death that has gripped our
nation. By deception the thief coaxes many to take
the wide road that leads to destruction. Forgive
your church for turning the abundant life which
you promised into a materialistic religion (seed
sown among thorns). Show us the U-turn that is
available and empower us to take it. Since death is
an enemy, let us fight it with the power that is
within us. In Jesus' Name, Amen!

July 12

"Let the little children come to me and do not hinder them, for to such belongs the kingdom of heaven."
(Matthew 19:14)

Heavenly Father, help us to see your heart towards the little ones through the eyes of Jesus, who being God the Son began his life in the human body prepared for him in the womb. What a powerful illustration this is of the fact that human life begins at the moment of conception. May this truth soon be written into the laws of our land, even as it is written in our hearts. In Jesus' Name, Amen!

July 13

"...now it is high time to awake out of sleep; for now our salvation is nearer than when we first believed. The night is far spent, the day is at hand. Therefore let us cast off the works of darkness, and let us put on the armor of light."
(Romans 13:11-12)

Almighty God, wake up your slumbering church. While we have much to rejoice about there is much that should cause us to roll up our sleeves and be about the Master's business. These are not mutually exclusive as we bring the Gospel message to the culture of death – saving lives; saving souls. In Jesus' Name, Amen!

July 14

"Whoever loves his life loses it, and whoever hates his life in this world will keep it for eternal life."
(John 12:25)

Ah Lord God, author and giver of life, may your church follow Your Son and our Lord's example of laying down our lives. Help us to do it as living sacrifices who forgo personal pleasure and comfort to rescue the lost, defend the weak, and speak for those with no voice. In Jesus' Name, Amen!

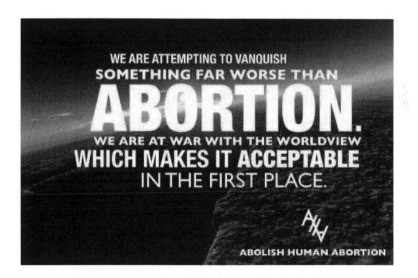

July 15

*"YODH Your hands have made and fashioned me;
give me understanding that I may learn your
commandments."*
(Psalms 119:73)

Heavenly Father, today I pray that I, along with
my brothers and sisters in Christ (and even the
nation) would gain understanding regarding the
fact that You are the Creator and we are the
created. As such may we bow to your will
concerning life, even life in the womb. May we
defend life and enact laws that do the same. In
Jesus' Name, Amen!

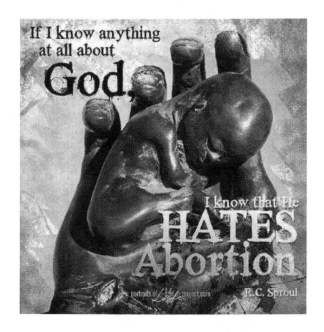

July 16

"When a scoffer is punished, the simple becomes wise; when a wise man is instructed, he gains knowledge."
(Proverbs 21:11)

Lord God, may all who claim to be wise listen to your instructions to choose life. In so doing they will gain knowledge and insight into the mystery of life. Such knowledge is so wonderful that it imparts an eternal perspective to the temporal. May such a perspective prevail in the land so that our laws and our attitudes would all be in defense of life. In Jesus' Name, Amen!

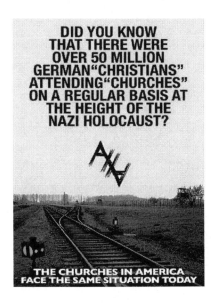

July 17

"Truly, truly, I say to you, whoever hears my word and believes him who sent me has eternal life. He does not come into judgment, but has passed from death to life."
(John 5:24)

Heavenly Father, we see all over your Word that life or death are choices. As much as you exhort us to choose life, and as much as you spell out the consequences of our choices, they are still choices. May we always choose life , even if it means laying down our lives for the benefit of others. In Jesus' Name, Amen!

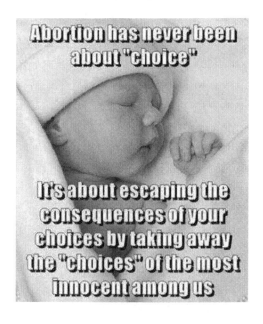

July 18

"Let them be put to shame and confusion who seek my life! Let them be turned back and brought to dishonor who delight in my hurt!"
(Psalm 70:2)

Dear God! We hear the psalmist crying out to you what could well be the cry of the unborn from the depths of the abortuaries. We join with them, asking that the horror of this genocide be seen for what it is and brought to a halt. In Jesus' Name. Amen!"

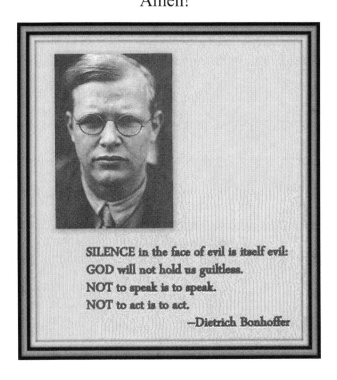

SILENCE in the face of evil is itself evil:
GOD will not hold us guiltless.
NOT to speak is to speak.
NOT to act is to act.
—Dietrich Bonhoffer

July 19

"And this is eternal life, that they know you the only true God, and Jesus Christ whom you have sent."
(John 17:3)

Our Father, You dwell in heaven. As we worship your Holy Name, we lament over the millions who thought that the only way to a better life was to sacrifice someone else's life. For every one of the 60 million aborted babies there are two parents who neglected eternal life and opted for a temporal fix. Call them to repentance, forgive them and heal them. Call your church to repentance for standing by and watching the status quo prevail. "No more!", we ask, in Jesus' Name, Amen!

ABORTION IS THE MOST EXTREME FORM OF BULLYING TAKING PLACE ON THIS PLANET.

ABOLISH **HUMAN** ABORTION

"You have made known to me the paths of life; you will make me full of gladness with your presence."
(Acts 2:28)

Heavenly Father, as we engage in the fight against abortion, please constantly remind us that we are engaged in a battle FOR life - the life of the baby and the spiritual lives of those involved in the abominable act. There are so many victims in this culture of death. Help us lead them all in the pathway of life, in Jesus' Name, Amen!

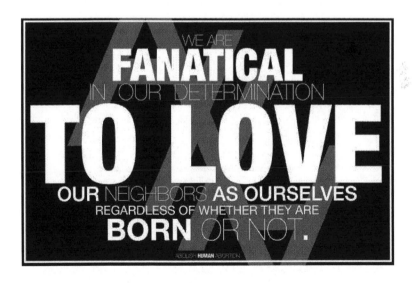

July 21

"Go therefore and make disciples of all nations,
baptizing them in the name of the Father and of the
Son and of the Holy Spirit, teaching them to
observe all that I have commanded you."
(Matthew 28:19-20)

Heavenly Father, it appears that our efforts to make converts are more successful than our efforts to make disciples. Certainly, You never taught us to kill our babies in the womb nor to sit idly by while others are doing it. You never taught us to forget the First Commandment. Forgive our neglect and apathy. May we once again become salt and light; promoters and defenders of life. In Jesus' Name, Amen!

July 22

"...nor is he served by human hands, as though he needed anything, since he himself gives to all mankind life and breath and everything."
(Acts 17:25)

Father God, since you give all mankind life and breath, who are we to take it away unjustly. Bring us to the realization of the obvious: pre-born babies are people, endowed by their creator with the same unalienable rights as the rest of us. When the law says otherwise, it is an unjust law. Grant us courage to resist and reform. In Jesus' Name, Amen!

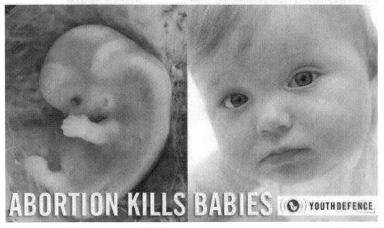

July 23

"But I do not account my life of any value nor as precious to myself, if only I may finish my course and the ministry that I received from the Lord Jesus, to testify to the gospel of the grace of God." (Act 20:24)

Heavenly Father, if your church had the attitude of Paul, surely we could overwhelm our congressmen with calls demanding passage of bills clarifying that the right of personhood under the 14th amendment begins at conception. Help us to realize that if we are to be a government of the people, by the people, and for the people, the people must speak up. In Jesus' Name, Amen!

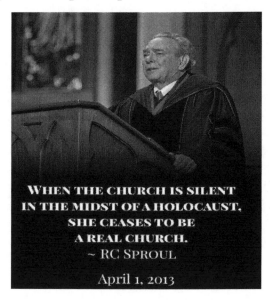

WHEN THE CHURCH IS SILENT
IN THE MIDST OF A HOLOCAUST,
SHE CEASES TO BE
A REAL CHURCH.
~ RC SPROUL

April 1, 2013

July 24

"When they heard these things they fell silent. And they glorified God, saying, "Then to the Gentiles also God has granted repentance that leads to life."
(Act 11:18)

Lord God, it is always repentance that leads to life: turning from the lusts of the flesh, the vanity of worldly philosophy, the pride of self, and turning to You. Open our eyes as individuals, as the church, and as a nation, to the need for repentance. May we turn to You and make a resounding choice for life. In Jesus' Name, Amen!

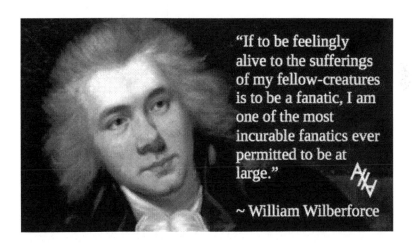

"If to be feelingly alive to the sufferings of my fellow-creatures is to be a fanatic, I am one of the most incurable fanatics ever permitted to be at large."

~ William Wilberforce

July 25

"But Paul went down and bent over him, and taking him in his arms, said, 'Do not be alarmed, for his life is in him.'"
(Acts 20:10)

God and Father of all life, just as this young man's life remained "in him," help the world to realize that life is in every baby from the moment of conception. It may not be any more detectable by sight than it was in this young man, but it is there none-the-less. May we submit to the fact that You, and You alone, should be the One to determine when life begins and when it ends. Blessed is the nation that does so, in Jesus' Name, Amen.

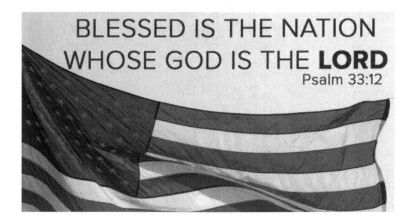

July 26

"Therefore, as one trespass led to condemnation for all men, so one act of righteousness leads to justification and life for all men."
(Rom 5:18)

Lord God Almighty, as we have all sinned in Adam, so we have all sinned personally. The good we know to do, we don't do; the bad we shouldn't do, we do. Thank You for grace that forgives us of wrongs and empowers us to do right. May your church become a force for good, a force for right, and a force for life, until Jesus comes and finishes the job. We pray in His Name, Amen!

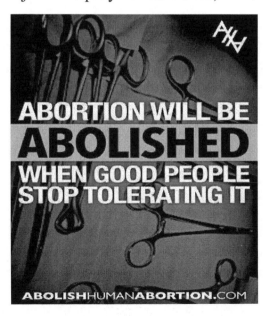

July 27

"We were buried therefore with him by baptism into death, in order that, just as Christ was raised from the dead by the glory of the Father, we too might walk in newness of life."
(Romans 6:4)

Lord God, You have rescued us from the deadness of our sins and trespasses and have raised us to newness of life. Prod us and empower us to rescue those who are being taken away to death. We cry out in their behalf as they have no voice of their own. May death be swallowed up in life, in Jesus' Name, Amen!

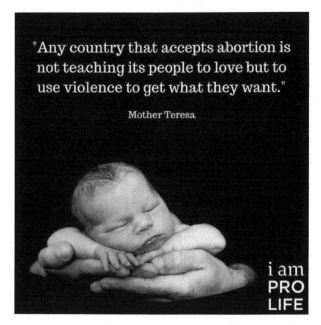

July 28

"For you know how, like a father with his children, we exhorted each one of you and encouraged you and charged you to walk in a manner worthy of God, who calls you into his own kingdom and glory."
(1 Thessalonians 2:11-12)

Heavenly Father, today we think of the millions of fathers who, willingly or otherwise, have had the privilege of fatherhood ripped from them by the sin of abortion. We pray for a dramatic turn of the father's hearts towards their children, and the children's hearts towards their fathers. In Jesus Name, Amen!

"Now therefore, be wise, O kings; Be instructed,
you judges of the earth. Serve the Lord with fear,
And rejoice with trembling."
(Psalms 2:10-11 NKJV)

Lord God, it is with sadness that we look around
and see the number of nations that have ignored
your admonishments in so many areas. Why do we
constantly think we know better than you do? And
this is not a complex political question; it is a
simple moral one. How long O Lord will You
allow us to murder the most innocent and helpless
among us with impunity? Turn us God, lest we be
consumed. In Jesus' Name, Amen!

July 30

"Do not present your members to sin as instruments for unrighteousness, but present yourselves to God as those who have been brought from death to life, and your members to God as instruments for righteousness."
(Romans 6:13)

Dear Lord, may we collectively and as individuals refrain from presenting our members to commit sin, either of omission or commission. Since life is a gift from you, may we be good stewards of life - our own and that of our neighbors. In Jesus' Name, Amen!

July 31

"while evil people and impostors will go on from bad to worse, deceiving and being deceived."
(2 Timothy 3:13)

Lord God Almighty, as You know we live in a time when the ancient Canaanite practice of child sacrifice is practiced throughout the world. And when Jesus returns He will judge in righteousness. May He find His Bride operating in faith, loving as He loves, and defending the oppressed. In Jesus' Name, Amen!

August 1

"2 For the law of the Spirit of life has set you free in Christ Jesus from the law of sin and death. ... 6 For to set the mind on the flesh is death, but to set the mind on the Spirit is life and peace."
(Romans 8:2, 6)

Lord God, deliver us we pray from the law of sin and death. We know that a changed mind is needed, and that only You can bring it to pass. Help us all, mothers and fathers, Christians and countrymen, to set our minds on the Spirit, and to thus enjoy life, liberty, and peace... In Jesus' Name, Amen!

*"And the angel said to her, 'Do not be afraid,
Mary, for you have found favor with God. And
behold, you will conceive in your womb and bear a
son, and you shall call his name Jesus.'"*
(Luke 1:30-31)

Heavenly Father, Your Word informs us that Your
Son and the Savior of the world began life at
conception in Mary's womb. If that doesn't
compel your church to defend life and to fight for
personhood laws, not much will. Cause us to will
and to do Your good pleasure. In Jesus' Name,
Amen!

August 3

"...who risked their necks for my life, to whom not only I give thanks but all the churches of the Gentiles give thanks as well."
(Romans 16:4)

YHWH, YHVH, Yehua, Jehovah - Thou art the Almighty One, the Great I Am. We see from your Word how you motivated people to risk their necks for the lives of others. May I be such a person, willing to do that which is both right and necessary to help bring an end to abortion in this country. In Jesus' Name, Amen!

August 4

*"For the law of the Spirit of life has set you free in
Christ Jesus from the law of sin and death."*
(Romans 8:2)

Lord, we understand that Jesus is all about life, and
that death is the last enemy to be defeated. As we
wait for Him to complete that work, may we, as
soldiers in His army, continue to fight for life, both
spiritual and natural - wherever the enemy would
try to kill, steal or destroy. In Jesus' Name, Amen!

August 5

"He lifts the poor from the dust and the needy from the garbage dump. He sets them among princes, even the princes of his own people!"
(Psalm 113:7-8 NLT)

Heavenly Father, during certain seasons, our attention is drawn to the graduation scene. At the same time we can't help but think about the 60 million plus people who have been denied an opportunity to learn and grow over the past 46 years. Some argue that many of them were aborted to save them from a life of misery and want. That is not our call! Our time and destiny should be submitted to Jesus, in whose Name we pray, Amen!

www.RememberingRoe.com

August 6

"Do you not know that we are to judge angels? How much more, then, matters pertaining to this life!"
(1Corinthians 6:3)

Almighty God, if this be true then why is your church so silent in judging matters pertaining to this life? We have your Word. Help us to rightly divide its truth. May the same Spirit that inspired the Word empower us to proclaim the Word. Your Word is spirit and it is LIFE. In Jesus' Name, Amen!

August 7

"Only let each person lead the life that the Lord has assigned to him, and to which God has called him..."
(1Corinthians 7:17)

Father God, we understand that just as there are different assignments within the church, there are also different assignments within the pro-life movement. We pray that everyone who calls themselves "Christian" will diligently seek out their assignment from You and engage in the fight for life. In Jesus' Name, Amen!

*"You foolish person! What you sow does not come
to life unless it dies."*
(1Corinthians 15:36)

Dear Lord, You seem to be telling us that unless
we are willing to allow a part of ourselves to die in
this fight for life, then death will prevail. Help us
to die to self: self-gratification, self-absorption,
self-importance. Help us to live for you first,
others second, and ourselves last. As self dies, our
lives come forth victoriously, even for the weakest
and most innocent among us. In Jesus' Name,
Amen!

August 9

"The Supreme Court, on June 26, 2018. ruled 5-4 in favor of pro-life crisis pregnancy centers in California, holding, in an opinion written by Justice Clarence Thomas, that a California law forcing them to post information on where to obtain abortions 'likely violates the First Amendment,'"

Lord God, Maker of heaven and earth, we rejoice in this small step in the right direction. At the same time we weep over the fact that babies in the womb are still denied the rights of personhood as delineated in the 14th Amendment of our Constitution. So, the rejoicing is limited as we must return to the battle. Life begins at conception and our laws should reflect that fact, in Jesus' Name, Amen!

"But if Christ is in you, although the body is dead because of sin, the Spirit is life because of righteousness."
(Romans 8:10 ESV)

Heavenly Father, we who make up your church, the Body of Christ, are changed; we are different; we are yours. Help us to be led by the Spirit, so that what we do in the body brings You honor. Arouse us to be defenders of the weak, a voice to the voiceless, and a source of hope to the hopeless, as we press on in the fight for life. In Jesus' Name, Amen!

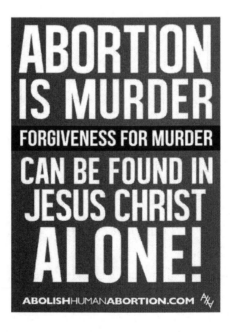

August 11

"Do you not know that we are to judge angels? How much more, then, matters pertaining to this life!"
(1Corinthians 6:3)

Lord God Almighty, may Your church arise with one voice and judge abortion for what it is - murder, the wrongful taking of an innocent life. Having so judged it, may we be moved to actions, ranging from prayer to passive resistance, to adoption. May these work to bring an end to the murder of the pre-born. In Jesus' Name, Amen!

"The good man out of the good treasure of his heart brings forth what is good; and the evil man out of the evil treasure brings forth what is evil; for his mouth speaks from that which fills his heart."
(Luke 6:45 NASB)

Most High God, it may have begun with a few voices who said in their hearts, "There is no God." How foolish, yet others have taken up the mantra and those who know the truth have remained silent. May our hearts embrace life as a gift so that our mouths speak for those who have no voice. In Jesus' Name, Amen!

"The silent and dormant church is the abortion industry's biggest ally. The abortion holocaust would end overnight if just a fraction of the nation's 500,000 churches became active in the fight."
- Mark Crutcher, Life Dynamics

August 13

"and on those parts of the body that we think less honorable we bestow the greater honor, and our unpresentable parts are treated with greater modesty,"
(1 Corinthians 12:23)

Father, just as the Body of Christ is made up of many members, so each one has a role in defending the gift of life. By Your grace, may each one of us find his or her role to play and then play it with all diligence, as unto the Lord. In Jesus' Name, Amen!

August 14

"The earth is given into the hand of the wicked: he covers the faces of the judges thereof; if not, where, [and] who [is] he?"
(Job 9:24)

Lord God, we have seen our land turned over to wickedness, and the hand that blind judges have had in the process - from removing prayer in schools, to legalizing abortion, to sanctifying same-sex marriage. We pray for opportunities to influence the restoration of righteous judgment in the land. May it be so. May our laws reflect what will one day be accomplished in You - death being swallowed up in life. In Jesus' Name, Amen!

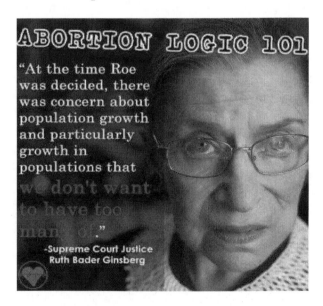

ABORTION LOGIC 101

"At the time Roe was decided, there was concern about population growth and particularly growth in populations that we don't want to have too many of."

-Supreme Court Justice Ruth Bader Ginsberg

August 15

"For we who live are always being given over to death for Jesus' sake, so that the life of Jesus also may be manifested in our mortal flesh."
(2Corinthians 4:11)

Eternal God, we are to die daily to self as we take up our crosses and follow Jesus as living sacrifices. There is always something we can do each day to advance the cause of life in behalf of those who cannot defend themselves. The first unalienable right belongs to the preborn as well as to us. May Jesus be manifested in our earthly lives, in Whose Name we pray, Amen!

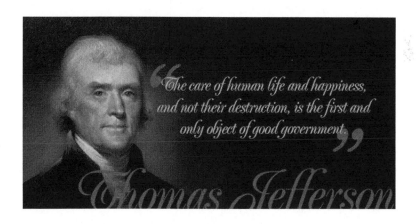

The care of human life and happiness, and not their destruction, is the first and only object of good government.

Thomas Jefferson

August 16

"Stand fast therefore in the liberty wherewith Christ has made us free, and be not entangled again with the yoke of bondage."
(Galatians 5:1)

Lord God, we thank you for the privilege of being a free people. Along with that freedom comes great responsibility. May we refuse to squander our liberties on things that only bring us under the yoke of sin again. Help us restore righteousness in the land and upon that may we truly build life, liberty, and justice for all. In Jesus' Name, Amen!

August 17

"I have been crucified with Christ. It is no longer I who live, but Christ who lives in me. And the life I now live in the flesh I live by faith in the Son of God, who loved me and gave himself for me."
(Galatians 2:20)

Heavenly Father, help us to see this Scripture as a reality in our lives. Help us then to ask the question, "What would Jesus do?" Then help us listen for the answer. Because Jesus is the whole Word become flesh, we won't find the answer just in the red letters. Help us to rightly divide the Word of truth, so that we may each know how and when to engage the battle for life. In Jesus' Name, Amen!

August 18

"So you shall put away the [guilt of] innocent blood from among you when you do [what is] right in the sight of the LORD."
(Deuteronomy 21:9 NKJV)

Lord God Almighty, here today in America, we speak often of American values. God forbid that the murder of innocent pre-born babies in the womb would be considered an American value. Forbid it Lord that over 1,000,000 men and women have died in combat so that we could kill off our posterity. Because life is an unalienable right from You, then we the people should do all to secure and protect that right. Help us Lord, in Jesus' Name, Amen.

August 19

"He will wipe away every tear from their eyes, and death shall be no more..."
(Revelation 21:4a)

Almighty God, in the perfect world which shall be our eternal abode, there is no more death. In this temporary world, infected by sin, death is an all too familiar occurrence. While it comes to all men eventually, we should never support or condone it happening at the very beginning of life. Help us to be clear in our understanding as followers of Christ – abortion must be abolished. In Jesus' Name, Amen!

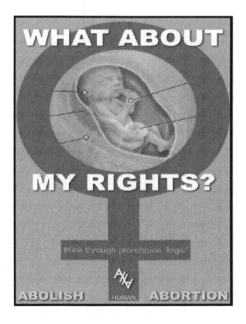

August 20

"They are darkened in their understanding, alienated from the life of God because of the ignorance that is in them, due to their hardness of heart."
(Ephesians 4:18)

Father God, before we say another word about "them" we confess that once we were "them." Thank you for the grace to know, understand, and act upon Your Truth. May the eyes of those who participate in, aid, or abet the murder of babies in the womb be opened. You have a magnificent way of turning enemies into advocates. In Jesus' Name, Amen!

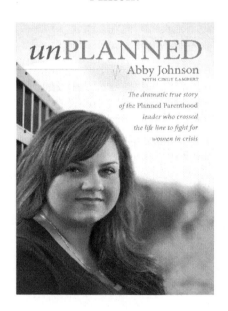

August 21

"They band together against the life of the
righteous and condemn the innocent to death."
(Psalm 94:21)

Father God, this verse describes the abortion
business to "T." Stir us up O' God to do what
everyone of us can do, because it requires a
commitment of no more than 3-4 minutes a month:
call our 3 congressmen demanding passage of
Personhood/Life at Conception bills. Lord, it is
such a simple way to overwhelm Washington with
demands for righteous laws. Help us to not be
discouraged by thoughts that our calls do not
count, in Jesus' Name, Amen!

August 22

"Only let your manner of life be worthy of the
gospel of Christ..."
(Philippians 1:27 ESV)

Heavenly Father, thank You for the way pro-life
warriors have been able to not only fight for the
life of the pre-born babies, but to fight for the
spiritual lives of the mothers, fathers, and abortion
workers. Thank you for the testimonies of lives
saved, both temporarily and eternally, in Jesus'
Name, Amen!

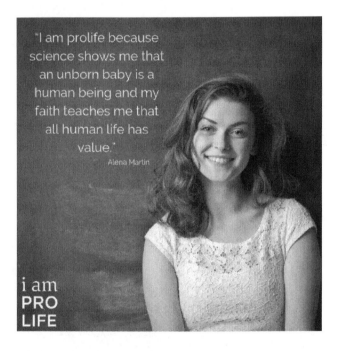

August 23

"...holding fast to the word of life, so that in the day of Christ I may be proud that I did not run in vain or labor in vain."
(Philippians 2:16 ESV)

Dear Lord, may we hold fast the word of life so that what we believe in our hearts may become the words of our mouths and the actions of our hands and feet. Life is a precious gift. May we who enjoy life do all we can to protect it, from the moment of conception. In Jesus' Name, Amen!

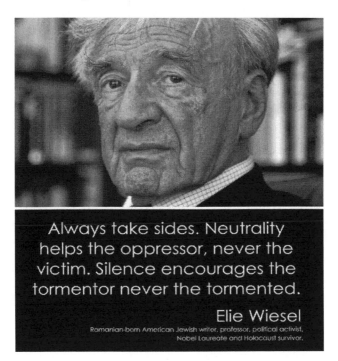

Always take sides. Neutrality helps the oppressor, never the victim. Silence encourages the tormentor never the tormented.

Elie Wiesel

Romanian-born American Jewish writer, professor, political activist, Nobel Laureate and Holocaust survivor.

August 24

"Blow the trumpet in Zion; consecrate a fast; call a solemn assembly..."
(Joel 2:15)

Lord God, You know those who pray to end abortion and those who call their congressmen demanding Personhood legislation. And You know the saints who hit the streets day in and day out, in all sorts of weather, risking the threat and even the actuality of arrest as they preach the Gospel on the sidewalks. Call others to the battle and grant everyone engaged in the battle for life the strength to persist until victory is won, in Jesus' Name. Amen!

"For you formed my inward parts; you knitted me together in my mother's womb."
(Psalm 139:13)

Father, Your Word declares that life is a divine gift and science proves when it begins. May we defend life from its earliest beginnings, because it is right and good. In Jesus' Name, Amen!

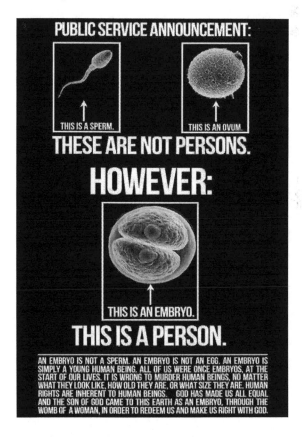

August 26

"For you have died, and your life is hidden with Christ in God."
(Colossians 3:3)

Father God, help us to see that when we engage in the battle for life, we are doing it by the power of the new man, hidden in you and empowered by the Holy Spirit. Help us to use every spiritual weapon available to us, even those that require anointed human effort - always giving thanks to God who gives us the victory through Jesus Christ our Lord, Amen!

August 27

"..for while bodily training is of some value, godliness is of value in every way, as it holds promise for the present life and also for the life to come."
(1Timothy 4:8)

Heavenly Father, whether I qualify as a heath or fitness addict, yet I am shamed when I spend more hours some days on physical (temporal) fitness than I do spiritual (eternal) fitness. Quicken me when that is about to happen. May I spend a proper balance of time in your Word, and in service to others... especially and including the unborn and all who would seek to end those precious lives. In Jesus' Name, Amen!

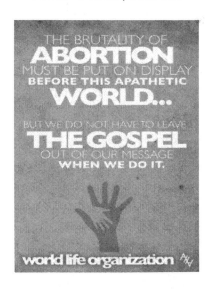

August 28

"Fight the good fight of the faith. Take hold of the eternal life to which you were called and about which you made the good confession in the presence of many witnesses"
(1Timothy 6:12)

Heavenly Father, we understand that the fight for life and justice is a fight of faith. We believe, based upon your Word, that life is a precious gift, and that the unjust taking of a life is an abomination to you. The world system however declares that abortion is a reproductive health care choice, while ignoring the slaughter of peaceful Christians of all ages in Nigeria. The challenges are big but You are BIGGER. So, we fight on, using weapons empowered by You to bring down strongholds. In Jesus' Name, Amen!

August 29

"Oh that you would slay the wicked, O God!
O men of blood, depart from me!"
(Psalm 139:19)

O Lord, hear this desperate cry. The wicked seem
to be winning, unless we look to You and the fact
that You will judge all things rightly, in Your own
time. So, help us to battle the sin while offering the
hope of the Gospel to the sinner, that life would be
victorious over death. In Jesus' Name, Amen!

August 30

"Indeed, all who desire to live a godly life in Christ Jesus will be persecuted"
(2Timothy 3:12)

Lord God Almighty, Captain of our salvation - strengthen us for the battle in these last days. May we be willing to suffer the persecution that invariably accompanies godly living. When we position ourselves between the potential victim and the potential murderer, we rely upon You and the weapons you provide for our protection and for the ultimate victory, in Jesus' Name, Amen!

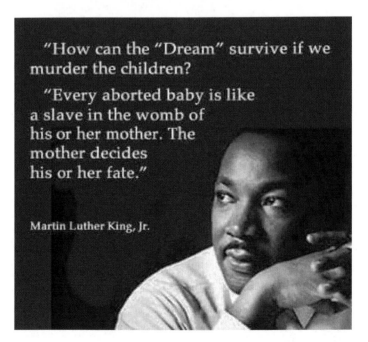

"How can the "Dream" survive if we murder the children?

"Every aborted baby is like a slave in the womb of his or her mother. The mother decides his or her fate."

Martin Luther King, Jr.

"...so that being justified by his grace we might become heirs according to the hope of eternal life." (Titus 3:7)

Father God, we thank you that Your grace and justification come to us as gifts from You. We don't engage in the fight for life trying to earn them, but because it is the right thing to do. It is the life of Christ in us and flowing through us, to set the captives free. Thank you for using us as instruments to save the innocent and to bring life to those dead in sins and trespasses. In Jesus Name. Amen!

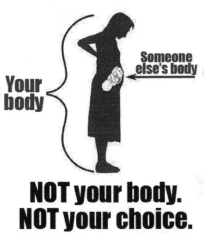

September 1

"No one who practices deceit shall dwell in my house; no one who utters lies shall continue before my eyes."
(Psalm 101:7)

Heavenly Father, we can see that deceiving the electorate has become big business in the USA. The church has expected the government to do her job, yet even with "conservative" majorities in both houses of congress and their man in the oval office, Personhood/Life at Conception bills have failed to get out of committee. Revive righteousness in the land we pray. In Jesus' Name, Amen!

IF YOU TRULY LOVE THE CHURCH, YOU WILL NOT LET HER REMAIN SLEEPING IN THE MIDST OF A HOLOCAUST.

September 2

"And for this reason God will send them strong delusion, that they should believe the lie, 12 that they all may be condemned who did not believe the truth but had pleasure in unrighteousness."
(2 Thessalonians 2:11-12 NKJV)

God of all creation, those who are beyond redemption is Your call, and yours alone. In the meantime, motivate and empower us to speak the truth, about the difference between right and wrong, life and death, truth and lies. May we bring You glory an all our efforts to defend life. In Jesus' Name, Amen!

George Orwell on Truth and Liberty

- The further a society drifts from the truth, the more it will hate those that speak it.

- If Liberty means anything at all, it means the right to tell people what they do not want to hear.

- Political language... is designed to make lies sound truthful and murder respectable, and give the appearance of solidity to pure wind.

- We have now sunk to a depth at which restatement of the obvious is the first duty of intelligent men.

- During times of universal deceit, telling the truth becomes a revolutionary act.

September 3

"For what have I to do with judging outsiders? Is it not those inside the church whom you are to judge?"
(1 Corinthians 5:12)

Lord God and Father of our Lord Jesus Christ, we can't expect the world to live up to biblical standards, especially if we in the church refuse to. We need to judge ourselves first, then make disciples. Help us to see that protecting the lives of babies in the womb is not just a biblical issue, but a constitutional issue. Even Paul was not above calling for the rights of Roman citizens to be respected. In Jesus' Name, Amen!

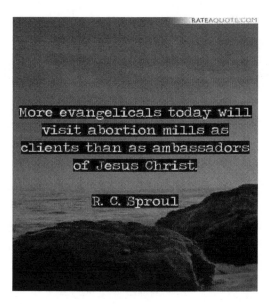

September 4

"Blessed is the man who remains steadfast under trial, for when he has stood the test he will receive the crown of life, which God has promised to those who love him."
(James 1:12)

Heavenly Father, it is indeed a trial to look around our world and view so much injustice. In our country, we the people are supposed to have a say in how things are done. May we so engage our elected representatives that they know, without a doubt, that a significant number of those who claim to be Christ-followers are demanding laws that protect life in the womb from the moment of conception. In Jesus' Name, Amen!

September 5

"And the LORD said, 'What have you done? The voice of your brother's blood is crying to me from the ground.'"
(Gen 4:10)

O LORD, in America alone, the voice of the blood of 60+ million slain babies is crying from the ground, and You are still saying, "What have you done?" We have made a few incremental changes. Help us to see that abortion isn't healthcare in need of regulation but genocide in need of abolition. In Jesus' Name, Amen!

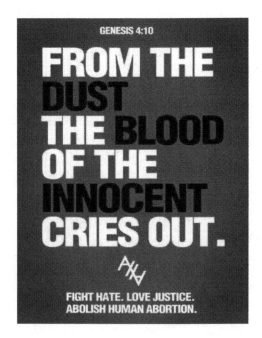

September 6

"And my God will supply every need of yours according to his riches in glory in Christ Jesus."
(Philippians 4:19)

Heavenly Father, you have given us all we need, including the Name of Jesus and the power of the Holy Spirit…all we need to be champions for life. Help us to use it for your glory, in Jesus' Name, Amen!

This is what we all looked like at 12 weeks in the womb. Legal to kill in all 50 states. Anyone think its not a person? Pass this along. It literally might save a life.

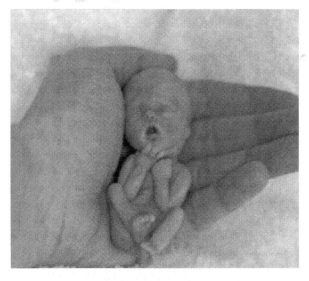

September 7

"For all that is in the world--the desires of the flesh and the desires of the eyes and pride of life-- is not from the Father but is from the world."
(1John 2:16)

Heavenly Father, we understand from Your Word that all sin is included categorically in these three. The sin of baby murder is no exception. May blind eyes be opened to this fact and may the grace of repentance come upon all who participate in. or are apathetic to this abomination. In Jesus' Name, Amen!

September 8

"We know that we have passed out of death into life, because we love the brothers. Whoever does not love abides in death."
(1John 3:14 ESV)

Father God, challenge us all with the questions, "Do you love your brothers? Even the least of them? How are you showing your love for them? Are you able to discern that I love all, even those engaged in the culture and business of death? Are you able to discern the many faces of my love? Are you willing to make sacrifices in defending life?" By Your grace, may we answer "Yes!" to them all, in Jesus' Name, Amen!

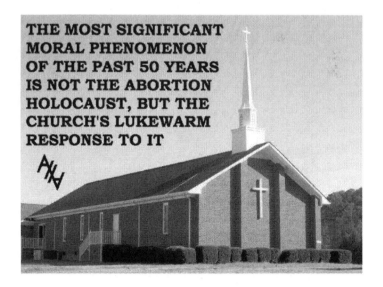

THE MOST SIGNIFICANT MORAL PHENOMENON OF THE PAST 50 YEARS IS NOT THE ABORTION HOLOCAUST, BUT THE CHURCH'S LUKEWARM RESPONSE TO IT

September 9

"...yet you do not know what tomorrow will bring. What is your life? For you are a mist that appears for a little time and then vanishes."
(James 4:14)

Lord God, considering how little time we get to spend in our mortal bodies, help us to number our days and to apply ourselves to wisdom. You say that he who wins souls is wise. At the abortion mills there is opportunity to save lives and souls both. Help us to shake off our complacency and to be about your business, for the night is coming when no man can work. In Jesus' Name, Amen!

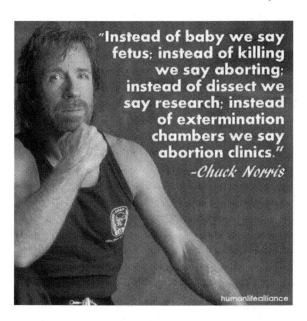

"Instead of baby we say fetus; instead of killing we say aborting; instead of dissect we say research; instead of extermination chambers we say abortion clinics."
-Chuck Norris

humanlifealliance

September 10

"His divine power has granted to us all things that pertain to life and godliness, through the knowledge of him who called us to his own glory and excellence,"
(2Peter 1:3)

Heavenly Father, considering this truth, how should we then live? What can we do to demonstrate your excellence and to bring You glory? Help us to remember that it is not always the things that we do in the spotlight that glorify You, but the things that we do for the least of these. You create life; may we glorify You in our efforts to protect it, even as we proclaim the message of eternal life, in Jesus Name, Amen!

September 11

"That which was from the beginning, which we have heard, which we have seen with our eyes, which we looked upon and have touched with our hands, concerning the word of life-- the life was made manifest, and we have seen it... "
(1John 1:1-2)

Heavenly Father, the life which was soon as Mary said to the heavenly made manifest to us was none other than the Lord Jesus Christ. He entered the world the same way we all do – from the womb of a woman. As we, with sorrow, remember all those lives lost on 9/22/01, may we also remember an equal number lost every day by the terror of abortion. Teach us to connect the dots so as to understand how precious life is, even from the moment of conception. In Jesus' Name, Amen!

Some facts to consider! Interestingly, more Americans were killed by abortionists on September 11 (about 3,200) than were killed by terrorists (about 3,000). Assuming 3,000 deaths among the 50,000 people who worked at the World Trade Center, about one in seventeen was killed. One in three unborn babies is killed by abortion every day. On September 11, it would have been six times safer to be a worker in the Twin Towers than it was to be a baby in his or her mother's womb. God created the womb of the mother to be the safest place for the development of life. It's 911 everyday for unborn children in America! We are 911Babies and we will not let you forget it!

www.911Babies.com

September 12

"...the life was made manifest, and we have seen it, and testify to it and proclaim to you the eternal life, which was with the Father and was made manifest to us--"
(1John 1:2)

Heavenly Father, today we again acknowledge that you revealed yourself to us in human flesh in the person of Jesus, and that He became human as an embryo in Mary's womb. What a strong affirmation of the value of life, from its earliest moments. May your church, all of us who will forever be indebted to Jesus, be strong defenders of life in His Name, Amen!

September 13

"For all that is in the world--the desires of the flesh and the desires of the eyes and pride of life-- is not from the Father but is from the world."
(1John 2:16)

Heavenly Father, the blight and reproach - yes the sin of abortion in this land, even in the world, stems from these three overarching temptations. Thank you that Jesus successfully resisted each one and in His sinless perfection died in our place on the cross. Now, in Him may we die to the flesh and join the fight for life, in Jesus' Name, Amen!

September 14

"We know that we have passed out of death into life, because we love the brothers. Whoever does not love abides in death."
(1John 3:14)

Dear Lord, cause us to check ourselves. Do we love others enough to go out of the way to share Your love with them? Are we bold enough in Jesus to proclaim the two-edged sword of both mercy and justice? Do we love life or just our own comfortable lives? Help us to love others, both those who are still under condemnation and the innocent who are being led to the slaughter. In Jesus' Name, Amen!

September 15

"Everyone who hates his brother is a murderer, and you know that no murderer has eternal life abiding in him."
(1John 3:15 ESV)

Heavenly Father, we know from Your Word that "hate" often means to "love something else more." May we understand our obligation to love You because You first loved us, and that our love for You is properly demonstrated in our love for others. May we not hate our brothers because we love ourselves more. Even if it is uncomfortable or inconvenient, may we show our love for You by loving "the least of these.." In Jesus' Name, Amen!

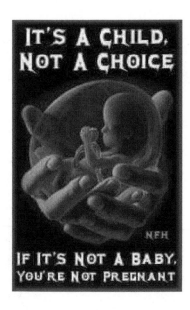

September 16

"And we know that the Son of God has come and has given us understanding, so that we may know him who is true; and we are in him who is true, in his Son Jesus Christ. He is the true God and eternal life."
(1John 5:20 ESV)

Lord God, you are the author and giver of life - both temporal and eternal. May we who have benefitted from both become champions of the former in defense of the defenseless, and champions of the latter that many might be set free from the lies of the devil. In Jesus' Name, Amen!

*"Whoever has the Son has life; whoever does not
have the Son of God does not have life."*
(1John 5:12)

Heavenly Father, forgive us for being consumed
with our own lives and the lives of people like us.
Forgive us for not seeing other lives - the dis-
enfranchised, the outcast, the downcast, the weak
and defenseless as being precious in your sight.
Stir our awareness and turn it into action.
Empower us to arise in ONE LOUD VOICE FOR
LIFE. In Jesus' Name, Amen!

September 18

"Do not fear what you are about to suffer. Behold, the devil is about to throw some of you into prison, that you may be tested, and for ten days you will have tribulation. Be faithful unto death, and I will give you the crown of life."
(Revelation 2:10)

Lord God, some of our Christian Brothers are facing the prospects of jail, even now, for standing up for the rights of the unborn. May we identify with their suffering and be willing to do so ourselves for righteousness sake. In Jesus'; Name, Amen!

September 19

"The beast that you saw was, and is not, and is about to rise from the bottomless pit and go to destruction. And the dwellers on earth whose names have not been written in the book of life from the foundation of the world will marvel to see the beast, because it was and is not and is to come."
(Revelation 17:8)

Lord God Almighty, keep us alert, watching, waiting, and faithfully doing Kingdom business, even up until that Day. You exhort us to run with the footmen now so that we can run with the chariots later. The whole abortion abomination is a battle ground. May we be engaged until victory is won. In Jesus' Name, Amen!

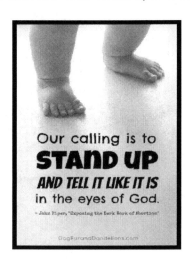

September 20

"And he said to me, 'it is done! I am the Alpha and the Omega, the beginning and the end. To the thirsty I will give from the spring of the water of life without payment.'"
(Revelation 21:6)

Lord God, life begins and ends with You. The Tree of Life, from which sinful man was banned, has been removed to the eternal New Jerusalem where the redeemed are invited to partake from it. You payed the price for this. Because of this we fear not the things which put pressure on life in the flesh. We commit ourselves to defend the defenseless, that they might experience physical life, and then, through faith, eternal life. In Jesus' Name, Amen!

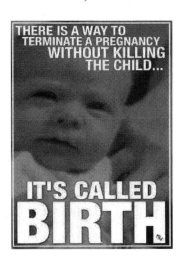

September 21

"...lest innocent blood be shed in your land that the LORD your God is giving you for an inheritance, and so the guilt of bloodshed be upon you."
(Deuteronomy 19:10)

Lord God, innocent blood has been shed in our land 60+ million times by abortion alone. We acknowledge that this is particularly heinous in your sight because of the defenselessness of the victims and the fact that it has been declared a legal right. Forgive us O God for ever letting this happen; forgive us for allowing it to continue for so long. There are multiple millions in this land that claim to be followers of your Son Jesus, so may we be stirred to rise up with one voice saying "Personhood to the unborn from the moment of conception." In Jesus' Name, Amen!

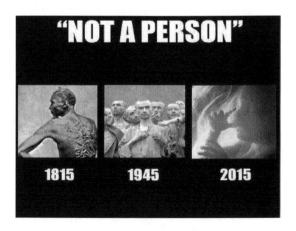

September 22

"So you shall purge the guilt of innocent blood from your midst, when you do what is right in the sight of the LORD."
(Deuteronomy 21:9)

Heavenly Father, how we have failed to purge the guilt of innocent blood from our midst. Forgive us of our tacit approval and our complacent complicity. Help us awaken to our responsibilities as Christ-followers; help us to not love the comfortable life, and help us do what is right. In Jesus' Name, Amen!

September 23

*"'Cursed be anyone who takes a bribe to shed
innocent blood.' And all the people shall say,
'Amen.'"*
(Deuteronomy 27:25)

Father God, we understand that outright payment
for such an abominable act is just as bad, and when
payment comes from the people via their
representative government, the curse comes upon
we the people. It is doubly bad when we the people
condone the act by allowing it to remain "legal."
Forgive us, O God and help us to repent. In Jesus'
Name, Amen!

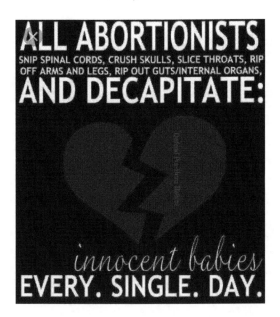

September 24

"...For he [Manasseh] filled Jerusalem with
innocent blood, and the LORD would not pardon."
(2Kings 24:4b)

Lord God, we are guilty of Manasseh's sin. How
self-righteous of us to pray and sing "God bless
America" when we have yet to repent. May we not
only have the grace to repent, but may we do so in
such a way that You are glorified and that the
world will know that You are the Creator, the Lord
and giver of Life. In Jesus Name, Amen!

September 25

"they poured out innocent blood, the blood of their sons and daughters, whom they sacrificed to the idols of Canaan, and the land was polluted with blood."
(Psalm 106:38)

Heavenly Father, we have done the same shameful things, if not directly, then with complicity because of our silence and apathy. How long can we continue this way and still You withhold Your judgment? May Your church judge herself and as the bride of the soon-coming King, so engage the battle as to avoid being judged with the world. In Jesus' Name, Amen!

September 26

"These six things the Lord hates, Yes, seven are an abomination to Him: A proud look, A lying tongue, Hands that shed innocent blood,"
(Proverbs 6:16-17)

YHWH Adonai, You Who are described as being LOVE hate certain things. To emulate your love, we must hate what You hate. Help us to hate with a holy hatred the shedding of innocent blood. Help us to see it for the abomination it truly is. Give us strategies to bring about its legal end in the land. In Jesus' Name, Amen!

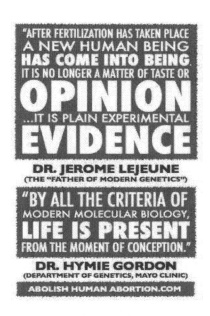

September 27

"Their feet run to evil, and they are swift to shed innocent blood; their thoughts are thoughts of iniquity; desolation and destruction are in their highways."
(Isaiah 59:7)

O God, how well your prophet, though writing 2700 years ago, described our country today. In fact, many countries share this ominous distinction. How we have despised the grace You have shed upon us. We keep praying 2 Chronicles 7:14 yet we do little to turn from our wicked apathy. Thank you for blessing our land, yet we wonder how long it will be until blessings are replaced by judgment. May we embrace Your ways rather than asking You to bless ours, in Jesus' Name, Amen!

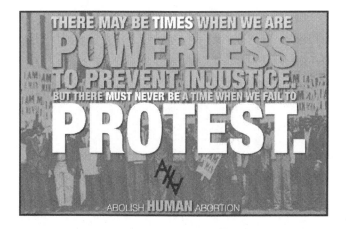

September 28

"Behold, children are a heritage from the LORD,
the fruit of the womb a reward."
(Psalm 127:3)

Heavenly Father, on this day when I remember my
own mother's birthday, I pray that all readers will
remember their own mothers. They gave us life.
May we use the gift wisely, that others might enjoy
the same gift, and one day find eternal life with
You. In Jesus' Name, Amen!

September 29

"Egypt shall become a desolation and Edom a desolate wilderness, for the violence done to the people of Judah, because they have shed innocent blood in their land."
(Joel 3:19)

Father God, it is abundantly clear from Your Word that judgment eventually comes upon the land of people who shed innocent blood. Forgive us if we, in our pride and arrogance, have declared ourselves exempt. Bring about a true repentance among your people so that the plague of abortion is removed from our land, in Jesus' Name, Amen!

"Being a Christian is less about cautiously avoiding sin than about courageously and actively doing God's will."

-DIETRICH BONHOEFFER

September 30

"If they say, 'Come with us, let us lie in wait for
blood; let us ambush the innocent without
reason;'"
(Proverbs 1:11)

Father God, if we were able, with fully developed
perception, to step into the tiny bodies of pre-born
babies, I'm sure we would view abortion as the
ambush of the innocent. Apparently natural man
has lost sight of this, and only by your spirit is it
revealed. Shake up those of us who see accurately
to act appropriately, and open the eyes of millions
who are blind to the truth. NO MORE
ABORTION, in Jesus' Name, Amen!

By not vigorously demanding the
abolition of abortion, the Church
shows contempt for the
commandment "thou shalt not
kill", pays more homage to an
unjust court opinion than to the
Holy Scriptures, and renders
unto Caesar a duty of conscience
owed exclusively to God.

ABORTION: Murder Renamed

The gifts of God ((Psalm 127:3)
They burn and they tear (Ezekiel 22:27)
Of God's righteous wrath
They have no fear (Romans 3:18)

They are of their father
His acts they'll perform. (John 8:44-45)
They murder our children
Before they are born

Confirming the warning
Of prophecy old
Their evil abounds
Their love now grown cold (Matthew 24:12)

The innocent slaughtered (Isaiah 59:7)
They call it choice
The wicked lay siege
On those with no voice (Isaiah 13:18)

God says they're persons
These words he has issued (Psalm 139:13-16)
But the murderous left ((Matthew 25:41)
Say they are just tissue

They hide behind terms (2 Peter 2:3)
Abortion and choice
To sugar coat murder ((Romans 16:18)
Of those with no voice

They're burned, ripped, and poisoned
And torn apart
By those with no conscience
And those with no hearts (Isaiah 13:18)

They murder these children
In wicked fashion
Even Sea Monsters
Show more compassion (Lamentations 4:3)

Oh that our words (Proverbs 18:21)
Might help end this slaughter
By calling these acts
Nothing but murder

Linen, M. (2018). Death Roe: State Funded Racism, Torture, and Murder. Unpublished manuscript.

October 1

"They band together against the life of the righteous and condemn the innocent to death."
(Psalm 94:21)

Lord God Almighty, we see that those who worked diligently to expose the atrocities within Planned Parenthood, that go beyond abortion, as the ones being prosecuted by our perverted justice system. We thank you that ultimately righteousness will triumph so we choose to be about Your business, even when it puts our lives in peril. May you soon vindicate all those who engage in the battle for life, in Jesus' Name, Amen!

"We've been very good at getting heart, lung, liver, because we know that I'm not going to crush that part. I'm going to basically crush below, I'm going to crush above, and I'm going to see if I can get it all intact."

— Debbie, Senior Director Medical Services, Planned Parenthood Federation of America

Planned Parenthood®

October 2

"Now Abimelech had not approached her. So he said, 'Lord, will you kill an innocent people?'"
(Genesis 20:4)

Lord God, You who do all things well answered that pray with an affirmative "No!" Why should we, Your people, sit idly by as innocent babies are killed to the tune of over 3,000 every day in America? We know that we shouldn't, so stir us to action to bring an end to "legalized" abortion in the land. No more death of the innocent, in Jesus' Name, Amen!

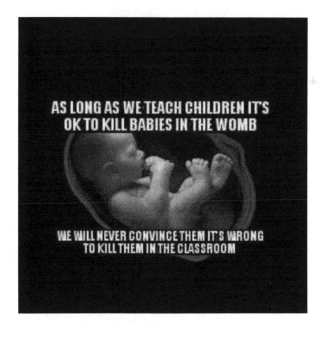

October 3

"When you serve as midwife to the Hebrew women and see them on the birthstool, if it is a son, you shall kill him, but if it is a daughter, she shall live."
(Exodus 1:16 ESV)

In many countries ultra-sound clinics abound, for the exact opposite purpose as stated in Exodus 1:16. In many cultures boys are preferred over girls, so if the ultrasound reveals a girl baby in the womb, she is murdered. Lord God, multiple millions of your image-bearers have been murdered while still in the womb, as sacrifices to the gods of convenience and preference. May we turn from our idolatry and return to You, the Lord and giver of life, in Jesus' Name, Amen!

> **"...I think future generations will look back at this history of our country and call us BARBARIANS for MURDERING millions of BABIES who we never gave a chance to live."**
>
> **Senator Marco Rubio**

October 4

"Then Moses called all the elders of Israel and said to them, 'Go and select lambs for yourselves according to your clans, and kill the Passover lamb.'"
(Exodus 12:21 ESV)

Lord God, Jesus has become our Passover Lamb and His shed blood is the full and satisfactory payment for our sins. As we find our life in Him, may we be moved to present Jesus the Messiah to others. May the Good News be used to draw many away from the deception that reproductive rights and women's choice have nothing to do with baby murder. Use us as instruments of light and life, all to Your glory. In Jesus' Name, Amen!

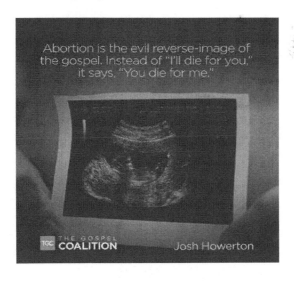

October 5

"Keep far from a false charge, and do not kill the innocent and righteous, for I will not acquit the wicked."
(Exodus 23:7 ESV)

Lord God, we kill on average 3000 innocent babies in the womb every day - and that with impunity. Except You keep a record and you will require an accounting. What a dreadful day that will be. May there be an outpouring of repentance by those who are called by your Name to such a degree that You will stay Your hand. Help us to bring an end to legalized abortion by the enactment of a righteous Personhood Law, in Jesus' Name, Amen!

October 6

*"They kill the widow and the sojourner, and
murder the fatherless;"*
(Psalm 94:6 ESV)

Heavenly Father, one portion of that verse stands
out in our present culture: "murder the fatherless."
So many of the babies murdered in the womb are
fatherless in a de facto sense. Fathers have either
abrogated their responsibilities or have had their
rights stripped from them by unjust laws. Father,
we cry out to you to correct these inequities, and to
restore the right to life that should be legally
recognized at conception. In Jesus' Name, Amen!

Heartbreaking. This man cried outside of a Planned
Parenthood facility because the mother of his child
was getting an abortion and he could do nothing
about it. Men do grieve abortion, and they often hurt
deeply because they are told they have no right to
defend the lives of their children.

October 7

"...because he did not kill me in the womb; so my mother would have been my grave, and her womb forever great."
(Jeremiah 20:17)

Lord God, we understand that it was You who formed Jeremiah in his mother's womb and it was You who called him to be a prophet to the nations even before he was born. What a tragedy it would have been if Jeremiah had been killed in his mother's womb. So it is with all babies killed in the womb, whether they have been called to be a prophet or a postman; a prince or a plumber. All life is precious and purposeful in your sight. May our actions and our laws reflect that, in Jesus' Name, Amen!

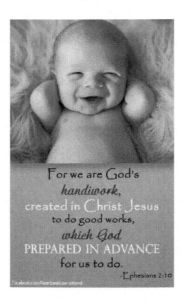

For we are God's
handiwork,
created in Christ Jesus
to do good works,
which God
PREPARED IN ADVANCE
for us to do.
-Ephesians 2:10

October 8

"Jeremiah said, "You shall not be given to them. Obey now the voice of the Lord in what I say to you, and it shall be well with you, and your life shall be spared."
(Jeremiah 38:20)

Almighty God and Father, it is well when life is spared. It was well for Jeremiah; it is well for us; and it is well for babies in the womb. May we not be so consumed with enjoying our lives that we neglect those whose lives are in danger. Mobilize us as the Army of the Lord, Defenders of Life, Protectors of those marching into the abortion mills. In Jesus' Name, Amen!

October 9

"And this is the judgment: the light has come into the world, and people loved the darkness rather than the light because their works were evil."
(John 3:19)

Heavenly Father, thank you for sending your Son and our Lord into the world. His life, death, burial, and resurrection bring life to all who believe and judgment to those who don't. In our fight to protect innocent babies in the womb, may we also bring the Gospel to those who are dead in their sins, ever mindful that we were once like them. In Jesus' Name, Amen!

October 10

"The thief comes only to steal and kill and destroy.
I came that they may have life and have it
abundantly."
(John 10:10)

Lord God Almighty, we see how abortion steals
the true joys of parenthood and childhood; kills the
unborn while they lie innocent and helpless in their
mother's womb; and destroys everything in its
wake. The foundation of the family is destroyed
and the effect of that is felt in the community, the
church, the state, and the nation - legitimatized by
de facto law and apathy. Help us to turn, and to
turn this around, in Jesus' Name, Amen!

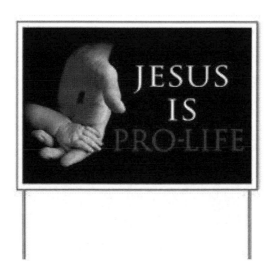

October 11

"For everyone who does wicked things hates the light and does not come to the light, lest his works should be exposed."
(John 3:20)

Most High God, Your Word is light and exposes our wicked deeds. We confess that we appreciate that, for only when we see our deeds as wicked are we moved to repent from them. May those involved directly in abortion repent. May those sitting complacently on the sidelines repent. May those giving legal authority to abortion repent. May those content with the darkness REPENT. In Jesus' Name, Amen!

October 12

*"And then the lawless one will be revealed, whom
the Lord Jesus will kill with the breath of his
mouth and bring to nothing by the appearance of
his coming."*
(2Thessalonians 2:8)

Lord God Almighty - as we look forward to that
day when Jesus returns to put all evil in its proper
place, we also long to see righteousness restored in
our land now. We cry out because the murder of
babies in the womb continues unabated. We mourn
because the destructive forces of evil have been
running rampant for more than 46 years. We plead
for empowering grace so that the legalized
shedding of innocent blood may cease in the land.
In Jesus' Name, Amen!

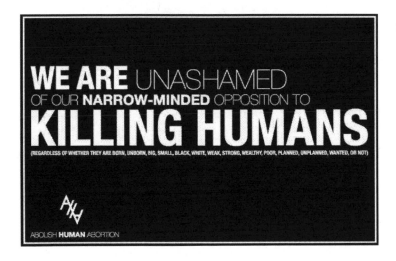

October 13

*"But whoever does what is true comes to the light,
so that it may be clearly seen that his works have
been carried out in God."*
(John 3:21)

Abba Father, is this why so many of the abortion
places are guarded by opaque barriers and have
few windows? Is this why they hire escorts to rush
"clients" inside lest they be exposed to the light? Is
this why the warriors for life pray and witness in
the clear light of day? Yes – may we all walk in
the light as you are in the light. In Jesus' Name,
Amen!

October 14

"May he defend the cause of the poor of the people, give deliverance to the children of the needy, and crush the oppressor!"
(Psalm 72:4)

Heavenly Father, Lord God Almighty! How we need you and your empowering grace to work in and through us to defend the children in the womb, and to bring the gospel to those who would even consider abortion something to be tolerated. May the conditions of 2 Chronicles 7:14 be satisfied so that You might come and heal our land. In Jesus' Name, Amen!

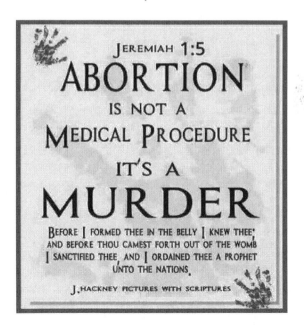

October 15

"And let us consider one another in order to stir up love and good works, not forsaking the assembling of ourselves together, as is the manner of some, but exhorting one another, and so much the more as you see the Day approaching."
(Hebrews 10:24-25 NKJV)

Father God, the signs are all around us that *the Day* is fast approaching. Night will soon be here when no man can work. So may your church arise and demonstrate love and good works in bringing about an end to legalized abortion in our land. In Jesus' Name, Amen!

October 16

"...they have grown fat and sleek. They know no bounds in deeds of evil; they judge not with justice the cause of the fatherless, to make it prosper, and they do not defend the rights of the needy."
(Jeremiah 5:28)

Father God, so it has become in the USA and in every country that has legalized the murder of babies in the womb (aka "abortion"). Forgive us for allowing this to happen and for doing so little to reverse it by the passage of just laws. Forgive our arrogance when we ask You to bless us despite those facts. The blood of 60MM+ souls still cries out to be avenged. May we pray and act accordingly, in Jesus' Name, Amen!

"...you who burn with lust among the oaks, under every green tree, who slaughter your children in the valleys, under the clefts of the rock."
(Isaiah 57:5)

Father God, while this Scripture doesn't describe the conditions surrounding every baby brought to the slaughter house, it is certainly the case of many. Eradicating legalized abortion will not necessarily create morality in the hearts of people, but it will restore a righteous foundation to our country. May it be so, even as your church arises to fulfill the Great Commission, in Jesus' Name, Amen!

October 18

*"He has pity on the weak and the needy, and saves
the lives of the needy."*
(Psalm 72:13)

Heavenly Father, there is none more weak and
needy than a baby in the womb of a mother who is
entering the killing field (euphemistically called a
women's health clinic). Your heart is to save such,
but like so many other things you expect your
church to act in the power of the Holy Spirit. Give
us strategies, strength, and even spunk to save the
needy. In Jesus' Name, Amen!

It is too late for me, but
Christian, please remember the
millions of my little brothers
and sisters whose lives are in
your hands.

October 19

"But my eyes are toward you, O GOD, my Lord; in you I seek refuge; leave me not defenseless!"
(Psalm 141:8 ESV)

Heavenly Father, as those created in Your image, babies in the womb innately look to You. Yet in the mysterious ways of love, You seldom exert Your will over and against others. So that leaves us, the ones who have responded to your saving grace, to be your ambassadors of reconciliation. Help us to do a better job of rescuing both the innocent and the guilty from the snares of abortion. In Jesus' Name, Amen!

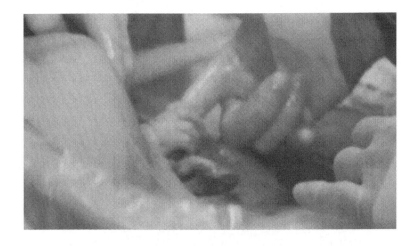

October 20

"An evildoer listens to wicked lips, and a liar gives ear to a mischievous tongue."
(Proverbs 17:4)

Lord God, history tells us that Hitler's propaganda minister, Joseph Goebbels, put the big lie into practice, saying: "If you tell a lie big enough and keep repeating it, people will eventually come to believe it." We have not only believed the lie - that babies in the womb are just blobs of flesh, a private part of a woman's body, and that she can do with it as she wishes – we have legalized it. Expose the lie for what it is and cause truth to triumph. In Jesus' Name, Amen!

October 21

"People who wink at wrong cause trouble, but a
bold reproof promotes peace."
(Proverbs 10:10 NLT)

Heavenly Father, we pray today for all those who
stand on the front lines, issuing bold reproofs
against the sin of pre-born baby murder. We thank
you for the millions who, over the years, have
heard the reproofs and turned from their wicked
ways. We thank you for the peace that comes when
life is embraced, especially when the One Who is
the Life is embraced as Lord and Messiah. In
Jesus' Name, Amen!

October 22

"He predestined us for adoption to himself as sons through Jesus Christ, according to the purpose of his will…"
(Ephesians 1:5)

Abba Father, we are so grateful that we have been adopted into your family through faith in the completed work of Your Son and our Lord, Jesus the Christ. May your church, and may the nations awaken to the blessings of adoption. May this be seen as the loving alternative to the murder of a baby in the womb. In Jesus' Name, Amen!

*"Rescue those who are being taken away to death;
hold back those who are stumbling to the
slaughter. If you say, "Behold, we did not know
this," does not he who weighs the heart perceive
it? Does not he who keeps watch over your soul
know it, and will he not repay man according to
his work?"*
(Proverbs 24:11-12)

Lord, we are without excuse. We know that
abortion is murder and we know that we have done
little to bring it to an end. Stir us from our lethargy
and empower us for the battle, lest we be found
guilty. In Jesus' Name, Amen!

October 24

This is a real-life departure from the normal format. This past week a precious baby was born to some dear friends of mine. The delivery held its own drama, but the baby was born, apparently quite healthy. A few quirks led to some tests which revealed the baby had an extremely low platelet count - so low that death was a possibility. Visiting that baby in the neo-natal ICU with two other pastors, the Word of God was spoken, followed, prayed, and believed. We left with a sense of internal peace, knowing that God would watch over His Word to perform it. In the meantime, medical personnel and science brought their best to bear. Today the baby was declared well and released to go home with his parents. Praise God. Through all this a stark contrast was evident. While great resources were used to save this baby's life, across town, in a poor excuse for a "women's health center" little babies were being murdered and discarded as medical waste with hardly the blink of an eye. Yet we know that God is the author and sustainer of life, so we continue to pray that death would be swallowed up in life, in Jesus' Name, Amen!

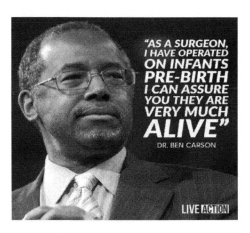

October 25

"And the LORD said to him, 'Pass through the city, through Jerusalem, and put a mark on the foreheads of the men who sigh and groan over all the abominations that are committed in it.'"
(Ezekiel 9:4)

Father God, who among your people are even sighing and groaning over the abominations being committed in our land, many with the blessing of our legal system? May you rouse us up to not only sigh and groan, but to issue forth a loud roar - such that the lawmakers will restore personhood rights to the unborn, in Jesus' Name, Amen!

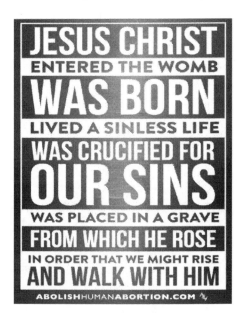

October 26

*"With respect to this they are surprised when you
do not join them in the same flood of debauchery,
and they malign you;"*
(1Peter 4:4)

Heavenly Father, we understand from the context
of this verse that Peter was exhorting the Christ-
follower to live the rest of his earthly life doing the
will of the Father. The last thing in the list of
things we are not to join the unbeliever in
practicing is lawless idolatry. The murder of babies
in the womb is the height of both lawlessness and
idolatry, according to Your Word. May your
church expose, reprove, and rebuke such acts of
rebellion against you, even as we offer your grace
to all. In Jesus' Name, Amen!

October 27

"But know this, that in the last days perilous times will come: For men will be lovers of themselves, lovers of money, boasters, proud, blasphemers, disobedient to parents, unthankful, unholy, unloving, unforgiving, slanderers, without self-control, brutal, despisers of good, traitors, headstrong, haughty, lovers of pleasure rather than lovers of God, having a form of godliness but denying its power. And from such people turn away!"
(2 Timothy 3:1-5)

Omnipotent God, it is obvious that the last days are upon us and this Scripture is being played out before our eyes. The personal sin of abortion has been a national sin for 46+ years now, and every trait described above could be applied to this sin. Is there any doubt that this sin is a root cause of all the other trouble and division plaguing our country, and even the world? May we robe ourselves in true godliness by virtue of the new birth, and take up the cause for life. In Jesus' Name, Amen!

An Abortionist is simply a paid Serial Killer
An Abortionist is simply a paid Serial Killer
An Abortionist is simply a paid Serial Killer

October 28

"The LORD is a stronghold for the oppressed, a stronghold in times of trouble."
(Psalm 9:9 ESV)

Lord God, this Scripture is why we bring the fight for life to the gates of the death camps disguised as women's health clinics. This is why we plead the cause of Personhood at the city gates (halls of congress in our case). We proclaim your Name, Your Gospel, and the judgment in which we all stand if we reject it. May we be used as instruments of salvation and eternal life, in Jesus' Name, Amen!

October 29

"Why do the nations rage, And the people plot a vain thing?"
(Psalms 2:1)

Almighty God, once our nation accepted an unjust court opinion, treating it as law, we were guilty of raging against You and of plotting a vain thing. In vain do we think we can be or become great while allowing the holocaust of abortion to continue these past 46+ years. You have set the precedent that such godless activity requires an accounting. Repentance from the blood-guilt is the only way to find mercy. Bring us to repentance, O Lord, that we might once again be a nation of righteousness. In Jesus' Name, Amen!

Righteousness exalts a nation, but sin is a reproach to any people.

~ Proverbs 14:34

October 30

"But you have eyes and heart only for your dishonest gain, for shedding innocent blood, and for practicing oppression and violence."
(Jeremiah 22:17)

Heavenly Father, some in our country shed innocent blood for dishonest gain; others promote the same; some actively participate, often deceived by the lies of the enemy. Then there is a huge number who turn away from such things, doing nothing to stop them. May this latter number decrease as your church arises and joins the battle for life (physical and spiritual). In Jesus' Name, Amen!

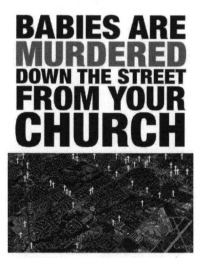

BABIES ARE MURDERED DOWN THE STREET FROM YOUR CHURCH

ABOLISH HUMAN ABORTION

October 31

"The first angel sounded: And hail and fire followed, mingled with blood, and they were thrown to the earth. And a third of the trees were burned up, and all green grass was burned up."
(Revelation 8:7)

Lord God, in recent months and years, fires have consumed untold amounts of land and hundreds of lives. Yet this is nothing like the coming fires of judgment. May we view limited catastrophes as warnings from You calling us to repentance, for You will judge all things righteously. In Jesus' Name, Amen!

November 1

*"O Lord my God, in You I put my trust; Save me
from all those who persecute me; And deliver me,
Lest they tear me like a lion, Rending me in pieces,
while there is none to deliver."*
(Psalms 7:1-2)

O Lord our God, in You do we put our trust.... but
what about the innocent babies in the womb who
are being led to slaughter today? Have we been
lulled to sleep because we've heard too many
"bless me" messages and too few about being
soldiers of the cross, willing to suffer persecution?
This Psalm describes in graphic detail what
happens to these little ones in the abortion mills
across the globe. Stir us to battle, O Lord of Hosts,
Inspire us to intervene with our prayers, voices,
hands, and feet... in Jesus' Name, Amen!

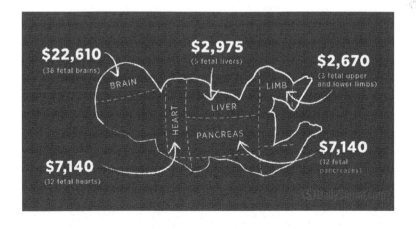

November 2

"Oh, let the wickedness of the wicked come to an end, But establish the just; For the righteous God tests the hearts and minds."
(Psalms 7:9)

Heavenly Father, bring the wickedness of abortion to an end we cry. Test our hearts and minds and help us to put feet, hands, and voices to our prayers, in Jesus' Name, Amen!

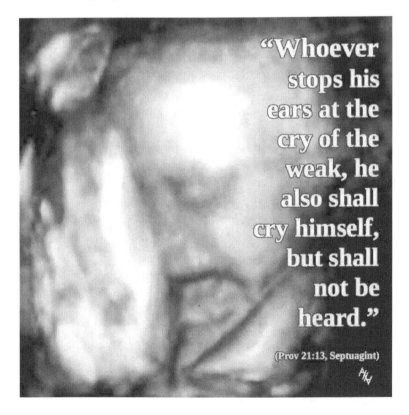

"Whoever stops his ears at the cry of the weak, he also shall cry himself, but shall not be heard."

(Prov 21:13, Septuagint)

November 3

"Out of the mouth of babes and nursing infants You have ordained strength, Because of Your enemies, That You may silence the enemy and the avenger."
(Psalms 8:2)

O Lord, our Lord, how majestic is Your Name! How precious are the babies to You, even from the moment of conception. As the Word became flesh when Mary said, "may it be to me as you have said" so it is with all human life - it begins at the moment of conception. May we shout that truth and champion that cause until it is the law of the land. In Jesus' Name, Amen!

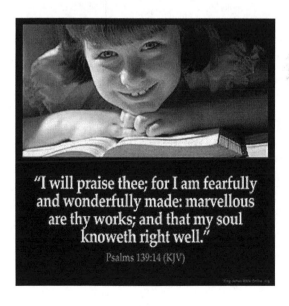

"I will praise thee; for I am fearfully and wonderfully made: marvellous are thy works; and that my soul knoweth right well."
Psalms 139:14 (KJV)

November 4

"Have mercy on me, O LORD! Consider my trouble from those who hate me, You who lift me up from the gates of death,"
(Psalm 9:13 NKJV)

Merciful God, we call upon You to lift up the pre-born from the gates of death. We know that You can do it at any time as an act of Your sovereign will, but Your love desires that we all respond to you with willing hearts. So may we be found willing, that you may use us to do your will - saving lives, ministering reconciliation, and restoring righteousness. In Jesus' Name, Amen!

Psalm 139:13

For you created my inmost being; you knit me together in my mother's womb.

November 5

"He [the wicked] sits in the lurking places of the villages; In the secret places he murders the innocent; His eyes are secretly fixed on the helpless."
(Psalm10:8)

Lord God, what an apt description that is of those who practice or are complicit in the practice of abortion. This is nothing less than the brutal murder of the most helpless among us. You have observed this for 46+ years being celebrated as a pseudo-constitutional exercise of the right of privacy. Help us to see through the deception and to break through the apathy. Help us end abortion by establishing the legal status of person to all, from the moment of conception until the moment of natural death. In Jesus' Name, Amen!

November 6

"God is a just judge, And God is angry with the wicked every day."
(Psalms 7:11)

Lord God, Your anger is just and righteous. The continued arrogance and apathy with respect to wickedness only breeds more anger until Your cup of wrath becomes full. You are a merciful God but Your mercy triumphs over justice only for those who, in repentance, desire it. May that desire loom large in us until our repentance results in actions to defend innocent life. May we cooperate with you to bring an end to the plague which haunts our land. In Jesus' Name, Amen!

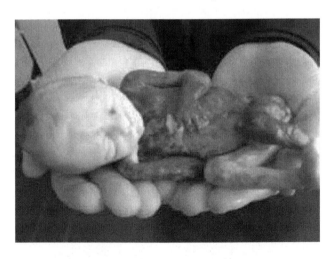

Baby aborted by saline injection

November 7

"Be not overcome of evil, but overcome evil with good."
(Romans 12:21)

Dear Lord, throughout the Scriptures You call to action those who believe. We are not supposed to be a royal priesthood sitting around a rapture waiting room, but a people showing "forth the praises of Him who has called us out of darkness into his marvelous light." We are called by Jesus "the light of the world" and that same Jesus says that if the light in us is darkness, how great is that darkness! Stir us to action Lord. By your grace may we act out our prayers and speak in behalf of those with no voice. In Jesus' Name, Amen!

November 8

"God brings nothing to the plans of nations, he foils the plans of the peoples. But the counsel of God stands forever, his heart's plans are for all generations. How blessed is the nation whose God is God, the people he chose as his heritage!"
(Psalm 33:10-12)

Lord God Almighty, how far America and the nations have fallen, and much of it is due to a self-centered church. May true revival come so that the church would again be described in the words of Acts 17:6 "These who have turned the world upside down are come here also." Abortion would end, and we would be, as Jesus described in the Sermon on the Mount, "salt of the earth." In His Name we pray, Amen!

November 9

*"God... from my mother's womb had set me apart
and called me through his grace"*
(Paul to the - Galatians 1:15)

Our God and our Father, this is just one of many
places in Your Word where You make it clear that
you are the Creator of life; that life begins at
conception; and that You determine purpose from
the womb. How arrogant of us to think that we can
ignore those truths and go our own way with You
never calling for an account. God have mercy on
us, whether our sins concerning baby killing be
those of commission or of omission. Grant us the
grace of repentance that we might be defenders of
life and the proclaimers of new life - in Jesus'
Name, Amen!

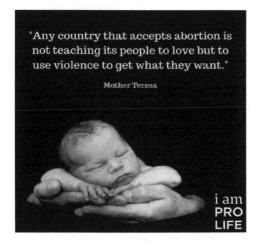

November 10

Three basic principles of life…

1. Human Life is sacred: *"Then God said, 'Let us make man in our image, after our likeness...'"* (Genesis 1:26)

2. There are only two genders: *"So God created man in his own image, in the image of God he created him; male and female he created them."* (Genesis 1:27)

3. The Divine plan of marriage is one man - one woman - for life: *"Therefore a man shall leave his father and his mother and hold fast to his wife, and they shall become one flesh."* (Genesis 2:24)

O God, considering what we have done in these three areas to poke our collective fingers in your eye, why wonder why there is so much violence and craziness in our society? May You restore righteousness. In Jesus' Name, Amen!

November 11

"The LORD tests the righteous, but his soul hates the wicked and the one who loves violence."
(Psalm 11:5)

Lord God Almighty, help us to see that the holocaust of abortion in our land has been, for the past 46+ years, a test for the righteous, and an open display (yes, even a celebration) of wickedness and violence. We, Your people who call upon Your Name, have, for the most part failed the test. Minor victories have been won to abate the violence, yet there has been no mass resistance. We have rights and responsibilities as citizens of two kingdoms. Help us O Lord, in Jesus' Name, Amen!

November 12

"On every side the wicked prowl, as vileness is exalted among the children of man."
(Psalm 12:8)

Dear Lord, we see this Scripture playing out in so many places: in the media, in entertainment, in the schools, on the streets, and even in our government. The poster child of it all seems to be the murder of babies in the womb. How we have come to despise the worth of human beings and the valor of defending the defenseless. Shake us O God out of our apathy; remove us from our comfort zones and cause us to be strong in the Lord and in the power of His might. In Jesus' Name, Amen!

"Have they no knowledge, all the evildoers who eat up my people as they eat bread and do not call upon the LORD? There they are in great terror, for God is with the generation of the righteous."
(Psalm 14:4-5)

Father in Heaven, there must be an innate knowledge that the ripping of a child, piece by piece, from its mother's womb is evil. Yet it is done with the casualness of eating a piece of bread by some. May the terror of what is being done, personally and nationally, be realized by us before it is too late to repent. In Jesus' Name, Amen.

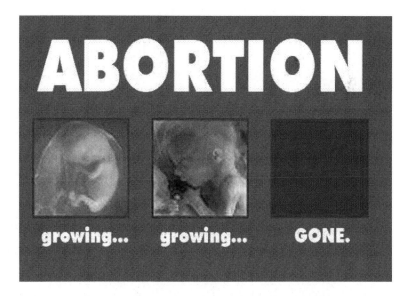

November 14

"If you have raced with men on foot, and they have wearied you, how will you compete with horses? And if in a safe land you are so trusting, what will you do in the thicket of the Jordan?"
(Jeremiah 12:5 ESV)

God Almighty, in your Word You continually warn and admonish Your people. You never judge us without first telling us what we should do and empowering us to do it. You also do nothing without first speaking it to Your Prophets. So Lord, how will your church be able to stand in the day of Great Tribulation when we don't even take a stand for the defenseless among us during times of relative peace? Awaken us O Lord; let the church militant arise so that in days future she might be the church at rest. In Jesus' Name, Amen!

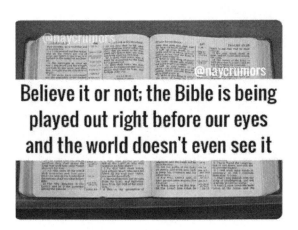

Believe it or not; the Bible is being played out right before our eyes and the world doesn't even see it

November 15

"You are the light of the world. A city set on a hill cannot be hidden. 15 Nor do people light a lamp and put it under a basket, but on a stand, and it gives light to all in the house. 16 In the same way, let your light shine before others, so that they may see your good works and give glory to your Father who is in heaven."
(Matthew 5:14-16)

Dear Lord, You have placed the light of Jesus within us. May we be obedient to this Scripture, being careful not to hide the light under the church steeple. May we shine the truth of your Word upon that which is evil and that which is good. May the light dispel the darkness of abortion. In Jesus' Name, Amen!

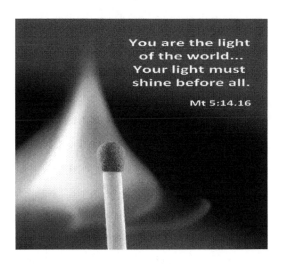

November 16

"... O LORD, who shall sojourn in your tent? Who shall dwell on your holy hill? 2 He who walks blamelessly and does what is right and speaks truth in his heart; 3 who does not slander with his tongue and does no evil to his neighbor, nor takes up a reproach against his friend; 4 in whose eyes a vile person is despised, but who honors those who fear the LORD"
(Psalm15:1-4a)

Lord God, so many of the Psalms speak of the sin of murdering babies in the womb, either directly or indirectly. This Psalm causes us to ask ourselves if we do what is right and speak truth. Do we do evil to our neighbor by not speaking up for them when they have no voice? Do we despise the vile people who support and practice abortion, or do we just ignore them? Help us to answer these questions and where your Spirit convicts us of falling short, may we be quickened by that same Spirit to act, in Jesus' Name, Amen!

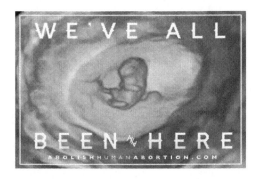

November 17

"The sorrows of those who run after another god shall multiply; their drink offerings of blood I will not pour out or take their names on my lips."
(Psalm 16:4 ESV)

Dear Lord, this is why we pray for personhood at conception to be the Law of the land. This is why we petition our congressmen. This is why we share the horrors of abortion to a world that acts as though they are unaware. This is why we witness in front of the abortion pits. This is why we work to protect innocent life and to bring the hope of new life to those caught up in the abomination - for whatever reason. Lord, bless all those on the front lines of the battle, and may the rear guard stay actively awake. May the Lord, the Giver of Life be glorified, in Jesus' Name, Amen!

November 18

"Keep me as the apple of your eye; hide me in the shadow of your wings, from the wicked who do me violence, my deadly enemies who surround me."
(Psalm 17:8-9 ESV)

Father God, we appeal to You today in behalf of all the pre-born babies who are in their mother's wombs. Each one is a person, created in Your image. May a desire for justice and righteousness to protect these little ones from murder trump the self-indulgent spirit in Your church. You patiently wait for men's laws to embrace Your precepts, but how long will You wait. May your church arise with one voice to say "NO to abortion!? and "YES to personhood!" If not us, who? If not now, when?
In Jesus' Name, Amen!

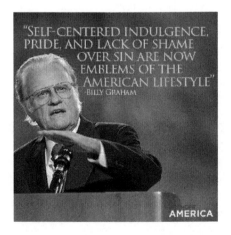

November 19

"I know your works: you are neither cold nor hot.
Would that you were either cold or hot! So,
because you are lukewarm, and neither hot nor
cold, I will spit you out of my mouth."
(Revelation 3:15-16)

Lord God, it seems that if we avoid asking ourselves whether we are lukewarm about You and Kingdom issues, we do so to our own peril. Can we be lukewarm about the sanctity of life without risking being spewn from your mouth? We dare not risk finding out. May we burn with a holy zeal in behalf of the pre-born's right to life, even as we preach the Gospel. Those who practice and procure abortions need salvation, no more and no less than anyone else. In Jesus' Name, Amen!

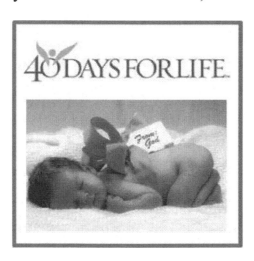

November 20

"The glory of young men/women is their strength, but the splendor of old men/women is their gray hair."
(Proverbs 20:29

Creator God, Maker of us all, may we see everyone, from the pre-born to those nearing the end of life, as valuable image-bearers of You. Cause Your entire church to rise and be a force for life… all for Your glory. In Jesus' Name, Amen!

November 21

"But thanks be to God, who gives us the victory through our Lord Jesus Christ."
(1 Corinthians 15:57)

Heavenly Father, thank you for revealing to us in Your Word that there are three enemies which we battle: the world (system), the devil, and the flesh. All three celebrate abortion. Thank you that we do not fight to attain victory, but we fight from the position of victory in Christ. Help us to display your victory in bringing about an end to abortion, in Jesus' Name, Amen!

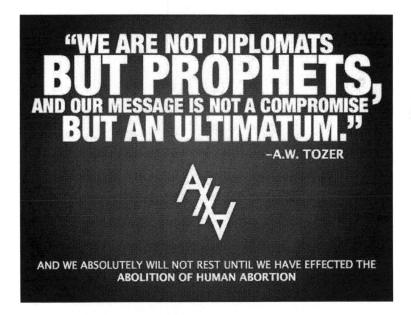

November 22

"When the righteous increase, the people rejoice,
but when the wicked rule, the people groan."
(Proverbs 29:2)

Almighty God, we are living in days when
wickedness seems to rule, and we groan. However,
we are not without hope. We know that all that is
in and of the world will pass away. Those who
mock you will either repent and be saved, or they
will be judged. May our righteousness in Christ be
on display, that many others will turn to You. In
Jesus' Name, Amen!

November 23

*"The King will answer and say to them,
'Assuredly, I say to you, inasmuch as you did it to
one of the least of these my brethren, you did it to
me.'"*
(Matthew 25:31-46)

Gracious and merciful Father, we renew our
dedication to defending the unborn and all whose
right to life is compromised by our godless
society's selfish lack of concern. Free us from our
own failures and sins so that we will be truly pro-
life in every area of our lives. In Jesus' Name,
Amen!

November 24

"Remember your Creator before the silver cord is loosed, or the golden bowl is broken, or the pitcher shattered at the fountain, or the wheel broken at the well. Then the dust will return to the earth as it was, and the spirit will return to God who gave it."
(Ecclesiastes 12:6-7)

O God, too often we try to live in ways that ignore our coming death. We forget that our days are numbered by You; that at the end of our days your judgment awaits; that You are the Lord of our destiny. Help us to repent daily, and then to live each day in joyful obedience. Lead us to live in the light and promise of eternity, fully and boldly proclaiming life. In Jesus' Name, Amen!

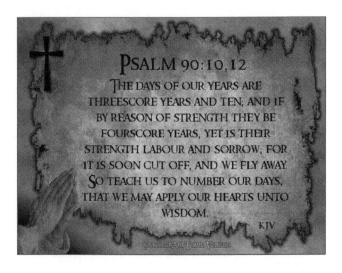

PSALM 90:10,12
THE DAYS OF OUR YEARS ARE THREESCORE YEARS AND TEN; AND IF BY REASON OF STRENGTH THEY BE FOURSCORE YEARS, YET IS THEIR STRENGTH LABOUR AND SORROW; FOR IT IS SOON CUT OFF, AND WE FLY AWAY. SO TEACH US TO NUMBER OUR DAYS, THAT WE MAY APPLY OUR HEARTS UNTO WISDOM.
KJV

November 25

"Yet I persistently sent to you all my servants the prophets, saying, 'Oh, do not do this abomination that I hate!'"
Jeremiah 44:4 (ESV)

Lord, You send some of us to places where the poorest, the most broken, the most captive, the most blind and the most oppressed in the world, are being participating in the abomination of abortion. Innocent babies are scheduled for destruction. Help us to bring them healing, liberty, life and justice through Jesus Christ our Lord, Amen.

November 26

"Rescue those who are being taken away to death; hold back those who are stumbling to the slaughter. If you say, "Behold, we did not know this," does not he who weighs the heart perceive it? Does not he who keeps watch over your soul know it, and will he not repay man according to his work?"
(Proverbs 24:11-12)

Heavenly Father, most of us have no grounds for saying that we do not know about those being taken away to death at the abortion mills. We can turn from the graphic signs and stop our ears to the cries to action, but it makes no difference. Lord, cause us to weigh our own hearts before You must do it. Embolden us, the church, to arise and say, "Abortion must end!" In Jesus' Name, Amen!

November 27

"have you not then made distinctions among yourselves and become judges with evil thoughts? ... 8 If you really fulfill the royal law according to the Scripture, "You shall love your neighbor as yourself," you are doing well.'"
(James 2:4,8)

Father, may you empower the hundreds today who are defending preborn life to effectively point out how discriminatory abortion often is. Help us to see that incremental regulation is also discriminatory. Grant us a bold spirit to proclaim the truth in love and perseverance. Empower the sidewalk prayer and witness warriors to not grow weary in well-doing. Encourage all who love Jesus to do something to stand up for life. In Jesus' Name, Amen!

November 28

"I beseech you to walk worthy of the calling with which you were called, with all lowliness, and gentleness, with longsuffering, bearing with one another in love."
(Ephesians 4:1b-2)

Dear Heavenly Father, we are humbled that you have called us and appointed us to be ambassadors of Christ in a world that is not our home. We pray that your Holy Spirit will empower us to walk worthy of the calling. We pray that Your unconditional love will flow through us to those who desperately need Your saving grace. Help us to be bold in the face of the culture of death, and to effectively deal with the tricky matter of trying to motivate the church to engage the battle. In Jesus' Name, Amen

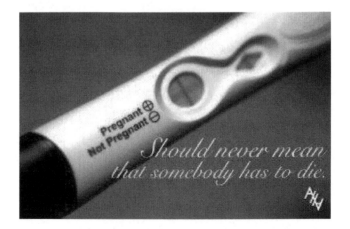

November 29

"My power is made perfect in weakness."
(2 Corinthians 12:9)

Lord, as we engage in the battle for life, we ask that everything in us that separates us from your perfect will would be pruned from our hearts and souls. In this blessed freedom may we experience a powerful anointing of your Holy Spirit. As we surrender the weakness of "what can one person do?" thinking to You, may Your strength bring effectiveness to our prayers, our sidewalk witness, and our calls to congressmen demanding passage of Personhood legislation. In Jesus' Name, Amen!

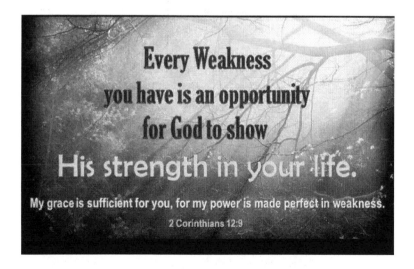

November 30

"A father of the fatherless, a defender of widows,
is God in His holy habitation."
(Psalm 68:5)

Heavenly Father, we thank you for caring about each of us so deeply. Help us to see and know you as our Father in heaven each and every day of our lives. Your loving hand also rests on every child today carried in its mother's womb. May they be born into this world and come to know fully and personally your endless love. In Jesus' Name, Amen!

December 1

"Let all bitterness, and wrath, and anger, and clamor, and evil speaking, be put away from you, with all malice. And be kind one to another, tenderhearted, forgiving one another, even as God for Christ's sake has forgiven you."
(Ephesians 4:31-32)

Dearest God, You tell us in Proverbs that the foolish and the wicked lack wisdom and understanding. We pray you would trouble the souls of those in the abortion industry and the souls of those who give them business, so that they might receive the above admonition. May they hunger for truth and cry out for freedom which can be found only in the Lord Jesus Christ, in Whose Name we pray. Amen!

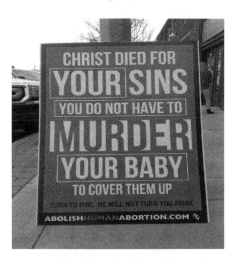

December 2

"but in your hearts honor Christ the Lord as holy, always being prepared to make a defense to anyone who asks you for a reason for the hope that is in you; yet do it with gentleness and respect,"
(1 Peter 3:15)

Heavenly Father, bless all of those today who take a public stand for life. Even in the face of opposition may they do it firmly, yet with gentleness and respect. Help all of the Pro-life warriors emulate Jesus, Who is the way, the truth, and the life. We pray in His precious Name, Amen!

December 3

"First of all, then, I urge that supplications, prayers, intercessions, and thanksgivings be made for all people, for kings and all who are in high positions, that we may lead a peaceful and quiet life, godly and dignified in every way."
(1 Timothy 2:1-2)

Lord God, may we regularly pray for those in authority, and may they use their authority in such a way that governments protect and defend the first unalienable right – life. Just as we prayed for Congressman Dr. Phil Roe, so we pray for all 535 of the US Congressmen, the President and the SCOTUS. In Jesus' Name, Amen!

December 4

"....and it came to pass, when they were in the field, that Cain rose up against Abel his brother and killed him. Then the Lord said to Cain, "Where is Abel your brother?" He said, 'I do not know. Am I my brother's keeper?."
(Genesis 4:8-9)

Father, help us to embrace the fact that we are our "brother's keeper." When, due to selfish motives, we try to cast off this responsibility please call us to account. Help us be pleasing to you and to our "brother" and help us to understand that the word "brother" knows no age, gender, racial or ethnic restrictions. Red and yellow, black and white, male and female, born and pre-born - they are all precious in your sight. They all receive life from you so may we be strong defenders of life. In Jesus' Name, Amen!

December 5

*"Come to me, all who labor and are heavy laden,
and I will give you rest."*
(Matthew 11:28)

Father, hear our prayer! Snatch desperate mothers
from the fire. Whatever pressure they are under,
whatever burdens they may be bearing, draw them
unto yourself and your rest. Bring them out of the
abortuaries and into the pregnancy help centers.
Deliver them from evil. Use us to help them
choose life and to see your hand of provision
which offers easy yokes, light burdens and
abundant LIFE. In Jesus' Name, Amen!

Throughout my pregnancy no one has ever asked: "When is your fetus due?"

December 6

"And the Lord God formed man of the dust of the ground, and breathed into his nostrils the breath of life; and man became a living being."
(Genesis 2:7)

Lord, we are yours. Thank you for breathing into us the breath of life. Thank you for claiming us as your own. May our words and actions in defense of human life proclaim to all the world that you alone are Lord of life and death, Lord of our freedom and of our choices. May we choose life, that we and our seed might live. In Jesus' Name, Amen!

December 7

"Behold, children are a heritage from the Lord... a reward. Like arrows in the hand of a warrior, so are the children of one's youth. Happy is the man who has his quiver full of them; they shall not be ashamed, ..."
(Psalm 127:3-5)

Heavenly Father, please keep us from taking for granted the gift of children. Help us to remember that this heritage You have given us begins at the moment of conception. Make us faithful stewards of these precious lives, that each generation might be raised in the nurture and admonition of the Lord. In Jesus' Name, Amen!

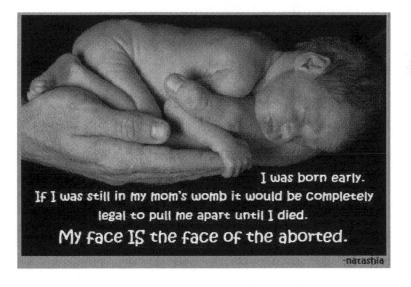

I was born early.
If I was still in my mom's womb it would be completely legal to pull me apart until I died.
My face IS the face of the aborted.

-natashia

December 8

"If I have despised the cause of my male or female servant when they complained against me, what then shall I do when God rises up? When He punishes, how shall I answer Him? Did not He who made me in the womb make them? Did not the same One fashion us in the womb?"
(Job 31:13-15)

God, forgive us when we try to explain away the obligation we have to help others who need help. Enable us to not devalue them because they are in the circumstance that they are in, but to see them for what they are. Like us, they were formed by Your hand in their mother's womb. That makes them valuable and precious. May we treat them as such. In Jesus' Name, Amen!

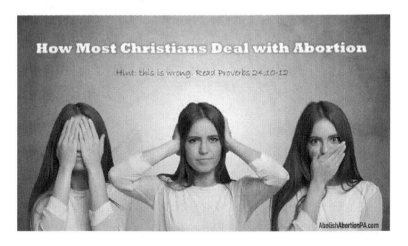

December 9

"Isaac prayed to the Lord for his wife because she was barren; the Lord granted his prayer and his wife conceived. The children struggled together within her, and she said, 'If it is thus, why do I live?' So she went to inquire of the Lord. And the Lord said to her, 'Two nations are in your womb, and two peoples, born of you, shall be divided; the one shall be stronger than the other, the elder shall serve the you.'"
(Genesis 25:21-23)

O, God, You formed us in our mother's womb and planned a unique and special life and purpose for each of us, and for that we thank you. Grant that we may tirelessly pray and work for an end to abortion, so that no unborn baby you have made may fail to achieve your divine intention for him or her because of intentional abortion. In Jesus' Name, Amen!

December 10

*"For we do not wrestle against flesh and blood,
but against principalities, against powers, against
the rulers of the darkness of this age, against
spiritual hosts of wickedness in the heavenly
places. Therefore, take up the whole armor of God,
that you may be able to withstand in the evil day
and having done all, to stand."*
(Ephesians 6:12-13

Dear Lord, as You lead us into the spiritual battle
of abortion may we be reminded that the battle is
truly Yours. Thank you for hearing our requests
for direction and protection. Thank you for the
victory that is ours because of Your Son Jesus, in
whom death is swallowed up in life, and in whose
Name we pray, Amen!

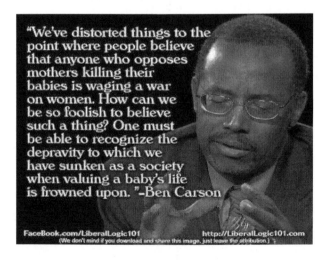

December 11

"Who among all these does not know that the hand of the Lord has done this, in His hand is the life of every creature and the breath of all mankind."
(Job 12:9-10)

Thank you, Father God, for being the Creator of every life. Please give me, and the society in which I live, an appreciation for your gift of life. Please help us set aside our pride and acknowledge that we need You. Show us how we can honor You today. As You do this may Your Spirit overflow into the lives of others, resulting in conviction, and an acceptance of Jesus as their righteousness, realizing that only in Him can anyone escape the judgment to come. In Jesus' Name, Amen!

December 12

"...then the Lord knows how to rescue the godly from trials, and to keep the unrighteous under punishment until the day of judgment..."
(2 Peter 2:9 ESV)

Yahweh Adonai, You certainly know that abortion is more than a USA sin, but a world-wide sin. In Munich an abortion mill is above a kindergarten. The abortionist once told prayer volunteers that he hopes they die of pneumonia, that he enjoys his work, and that he is training his son to follow in his footsteps. He has boasted about performing up to 20 abortions a day. Many of his abortions are performed when the babies are in their 3rd trimester. Is it any wonder that The Day of the Lord will be a time of judgment for the whole earth? May we be found faithful on that day. In Jesus' Name, Amen!

December 13

"But the Lord said 'You have had pity on the plant for which you have not labored, nor made it grow, which came up in the night and perished in the night. And should I not pity Nineveh, that great city, in which are more than one hundred and twenty thousand persons who cannot discern between their right hand and their left, and much livestock? Should I not be concerned about that great city?'"
(Jonah 4:10-11)

Gracious God, loving our enemies seems like one of most difficult things you could ask of us. Please remind us that this is how you love and that if you ask it of us then you will give us the grace to do it. Empower us to know and to do the work of evangelism , proclaiming Your truth in love, which, by that same grace, leads some to repentance. In Jesus' Name, Amen!

December 14

"Now these are Your servants and Your people, whom You have redeemed by Your great power, and by Your strong hand. O Lord, please let Your ear be attentive to the prayer of Your servants who desire to fear Your name."
(Nehemiah 1:10-11)

We pray for your continued guidance and protection as we daily work to defend life. May we be steadfast, unmovable, always abounding in Your work, knowing that our labor will not be in vain. Give us vision to see that life isn't just about now, but it is generational. In Jesus' Name, Amen!

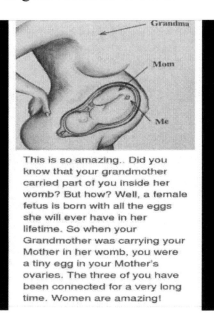

This is so amazing.. Did you know that your grandmother carried part of you inside her womb? But how? Well, a female fetus is born with all the eggs she will ever have in her lifetime. So when your Grandmother was carrying your Mother in her womb, you were a tiny egg in your Mother's ovaries. The three of you have been connected for a very long time. Women are amazing!

December 15

"Then the word of the Lord came to me, saying:
'Before I formed you in the womb I knew you;
Before you were born I sanctified you; I ordained
you a prophet to the nations.'"
(Jeremiah 1:4-5)

O Lord, we confess that in You we live and move
and have our being. Because You are, we are. May
we find grace from You to affirm the being of
every human, beginning at conception. May we
labor to make this truth known to the world around
us. Let this truth be expressed in equal protection
and justice under our laws. In Jesus' Name, Amen!

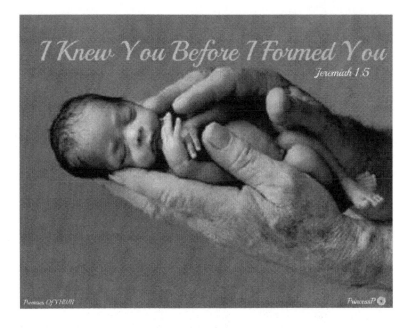

December 16

"These all wait for you, that you may give them their food in due season, what you give them they gather in; you open your hand they are filled with good. You hide your face, they are troubled; you take away their breath, they die and return to their dust. You send forth your Spirit, they are created; and you renew the face of the earth."
(Psalm 104:27-30)

Beloved Father, remind us today that there is no truth but You. Do not let us fall prey to the evil one's lie that the choice of death brings with it no pain or regret. Remind us right now that You who created all life also sustain all life. Let us choose life always and enable us to effectively encourage others to do likewise. In Jesus' Name, Amen!

December 17

"Let this mind be in you which was also in Christ Jesus, who being in the form of God did not consider it robbery to be equal with God, but made Himself of no reputation, taking the form of a bondservant, and coming in the likeness of men. And being found in appearance as a man, He humbled himself and became obedient to the point of death, even the death of the cross."
(Philippians 2:5-8)

Lord, help us follow in the footsteps of Jesus. Let us humbly and diligently work to restore legal protection for the unborn, the disabled, the medically dependent and all innocent children of God whose lives are threatened. Let us remember the old adage that "He can never lead who has not first learned to obey." And Lord, grant us obedient hearts as we labor in your name. Amen!

Jesus is Pro-life

Take heed that ye despise not one of these little ones; for I say unto you, That in heaven their angels do always behold the face of my Father which is in heaven.

Matthew 18:10

www.facebook.com/avoiceforhope

December 18

"Wash yourselves, make yourselves clean; Put away the evil of your doings from before My eyes. Cease to do evil, learn to do good; seek justice, rebuke the oppressor; defend the fatherless, plead for the widow."
(Isaiah 1:16-17)

O God, our heavenly Father, give us courage and wisdom as we seek to eradicate the evil of abortion in our society. Help us to realize that your divine Spirit alone can change hearts and minds, even within the church. We pray that all your human creatures may enjoy the fullness of life you intended for them. In Jesus' Name, Amen!

December 19

"Who is a God like You, pardoning iniquity and passing over the transgressions of the remnant of His heritage? He does not retain His anger forever, because He delights in mercy. He will again have compassion on us; and will subdue our iniquities." (Micah 7:18-19)

Hear our prayer of repentance, Lord, and cleanse us from all unrighteousness. It is only by Your grace that we can live lives that are just, and merciful. May Your Holy Spirit enable us to walk humbly in Your presence and may You be pleased to restore our nation so that a generation not yet born may praise you. In Jesus' Name, Amen!

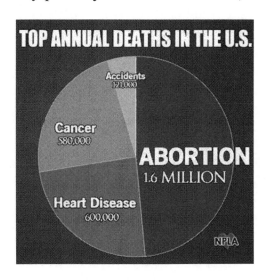

December 20

"Your eyes saw my substance, being yet unformed. And in Your Book, they all were written, the days fashioned for me, when as yet there were none of them."
(Psalm 139:16)

Gracious God, help us to appreciate the wonder and beauty of Your creation. Help us proclaim, on behalf of every one of our fellow human beings, "I am fearfully and wonderfully made." May the knowledge that we are intimately known by You shape our lives and actions. And for those who faithfully gather at the killing places, day after day, offering counsel and making intercessions, bless them to see a harvest of righteousness, in Jesus' Name, Amen!

December 21

"How can you say, 'We are wise, and the law of the LORD is with us'? But behold, the lying pen of the scribes has made it into a lie. ... from the least to the greatest everyone is greedy for unjust gain; from prophet to priest, everyone deals falsely."
(Jeremiah 8:8, 10)

Holy God, we have made a mockery of your commandments and have labeled abominations as blessings. As judgment begins at the house of the Lord, may Your people arise and proclaim truth and righteousness, even with our last breath. In Jesus' Name, Amen!

December 22

"About three months later Judah was told, "Tamar your daughter-in-law has been immoral. Moreover, she is pregnant by immorality." And Judah said, "Bring her out, and let her be burned.'" (Genesis 38:24)

O God, regardless of the circumstances of conception, every baby is valuable in your sight. The offspring of Tamar as a result of immoral intercourse with her father-in-law was Perez, listed in the genealogy of Jesus. May we never discount your ability to wonderfully use any life in fulfillment of your plans. Stir your people to labor, so that personhood rights would extend to all unborn humans with no exceptions. In Jesus' Name, Amen!

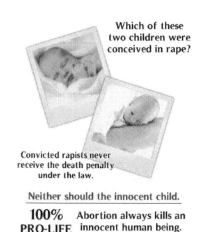

Which of these two children were conceived in rape?

Convicted rapists never receive the death penalty under the law.

Neither should the innocent child.

100% PRO-LIFE Abortion always kills an innocent human being.

www.facebook.com/avoiceforhope

December 23

"When I consider Your heavens, the work of Your fingers, the moon and the stars, which You have ordained, what is man that You are mindful of him, and the son of man that You visit him? For You have made him a little lower than the angels, and You have crowned him with glory and honor."
(Psalm 8:3-9)

Lord, you are the creator of all things. Guide my thoughts to consider your creation in all of its majesty, beauty and holiness. Guide my heart concerning your creation of precious human life. Help me to comprehend how essential life is in your own heart; to appreciate, love and protect all human life, so that I would step out of my comfort zone to bring about an end to "legalized" abortion.
In Jesus' Name, Amen!

December 24

"And the angel said to her, "Do not be afraid, Mary, for you have found favor with God. 31 And behold, you will conceive in your womb and bear a son, and you shall call his name Jesus."
(Luke 1:30-31)

Heavenly Father, you have made the womb of each woman a very special place. Help us to hold fast to the sanctity of this first home of humanity, remembering the wonderful mystery, that God inhabited the womb of a young woman and came forth as the savior and deliverer of the world. In Jesus' Name, Amen!

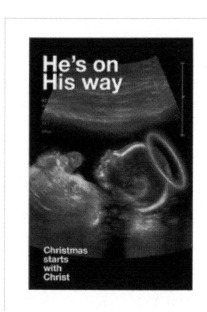

December 25

"For unto you is born this day in the city of David a Savior, who is Christ the Lord. 12 And this will be a sign for you: you will find a baby wrapped in swaddling cloths and lying in a manger."
(Luke 2:11-12)

Good and gracious God, we thank you for send us Your Son; that through faith in His life, death, and resurrection, we might be restored to right relationship with You. May the joy of this new life so infuse Your church that she would proclaim the Gospel to all, even at the abortion mills. Your grace not only delivers us from the penalty of sin but from the power of sin. In Jesus' Name, Amen!

December 26

"Blessed be the God and Father of our Lord Jesus Christ, who…In love… predestined us for adoption to himself as sons through Jesus Christ, according to the purpose of his will…"
(Ephesians 1:3-5)

Father God, only You could see that when this picture was taken on 10/2/1994 that 20 months later the young lady here was pointing to the woman who would become her mother through adoption. That woman is my wife and we were and continue to be blessed by our daughter. A new generation of beautiful people are now part of our family. Adoption is indeed the Loving Option. In Jesus' Name, Amen!

December 27

"Blessed are those whose lawless deeds are forgiven, and whose sin is covered. Blessed is the one to whom the Lord shall not impute sin."
(Romans 4:7-8)

Our Most Gracious Heavenly Father, thank you for your amazing grace that saved a wretch like me. I come against the enemy of my soul who would have me feel cast down and dejected. Lord, keep your children from falling prey to the accusations of the father of lies. Turn our mourning into dancing and may we bring praise to you as we give testimony of Your healing and restoration in our lives. And may that testimony translate into righteous laws which recognize that life begins at conception. In Jesus' Name, Amen!

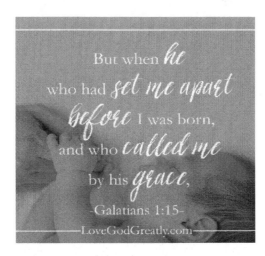

But when *he* who had *set me apart before* I was born, and who *called me* by his *grace,*
Galatians 1:15
LoveGodGreatly.com

December 28

"God created man in His own image, in the image of God He created him, male and female He created them. And God said to them, 'Be fruitful and multiply...'"
(Genesis 1:27-28a)

Father of mercy and grace, we thank you for the gift of our children. Grant that every fiber of our being may rejoice when a new baby, our own or anyone else's, is born into the world. Help us to welcome them as we would welcome you, for whenever a new baby is conceived, another life to bear your image and another voice to praise and worship you is beginning. In Jesus' Name, Amen!

"See, I have engraved you on the palms of MY hands; your walls are ever before ME."
Isaiah 49:16

December 29

"I beseech you therefore brethren, by the mercies of God, that you present your bodies a living sacrifice, holy, acceptable to God, which is your reasonable service."
(Romans 12:1)

God Almighty, You alone are worthy of our praise and worship. Anyone may accept Your Son's sacrifice in their behalf and in turn present their bodies to you as living sacrifices. I pray that you would use them and me as your vessels to rescue others who are perishing, whether it be in the sin of abortion or by the sin of abortion. In Jesus' Name, Amen!

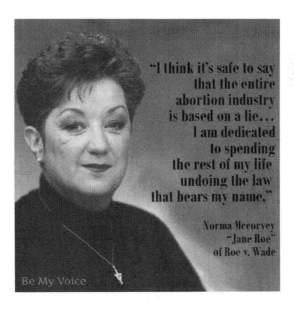

"When they heard these things they fell silent. And they glorified God, saying, 'Then to the Gentiles also God has granted repentance that leads to life.'"
(Acts 11:18)

Merciful God, none of us praying to end abortion do it from a position of moral superiority. Rather we thank you that the same repentance that was granted to us is available to anyone. May those caught up in the deception of sin, personally or corporately, be granted repentance to reject death and embrace life. In Jesus' Name, Amen!

WHOEVER CONCEALS HIS TRANSGRESSIONS
WILL NOT PROSPER
BUT HE WHO CONFESSES AND FORSAKES THEM
WILL OBTAIN MERCY
—— PROVERBS 28:13 ——

December 31

"He will wipe every tear from their eyes. There will be no more death or mourning or crying or pain, for the old order of things has passed away. He who was seated on the throne said, 'I am making everything new!'"
(Revelation 21:4-5)

Father, you are the God of hope. Your word fills us with the vision of the world to come, when every tear will be wiped away, and death will be no more. Father, how we need that hope; how we are strengthened by that vision! Keep our hearts focused on heaven, and diligent in the labors of earth. As we struggle against the culture of death, root our souls in the assurance of victory. In Jesus' Name, Amen!

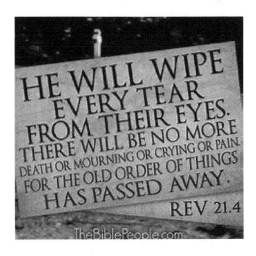

EPILOGUE

The Cause

There is much work to be done to restore righteousness to our land. The number one priority should be for government to do what it was established to do – defend the unalienable rights of its citizens. The first such right, endowed to us by the Creator, is LIFE!

"And David said, "What have I done now? Is there not a cause?" 1 Samuel 17:29 (NKJV) Yes! There is a cause and it is life - the life of everyone made in God's image, from the moment of conception until the moment of natural death. Our nation was founded on the basic principle that life is an inalienable right, given by God. Yet we have become a nation that has legalized the murder of over 60 MILLION innocent lives under the guise of "choice" and "privacy."

The 14th Amendment, Section 1. "All persons born or naturalized in the United States and subject to the jurisdiction thereof are citizens of the United States and of the State wherein they reside. No State shall make or enforce any law which shall abridge the privileges or immunities of citizens of the United States; nor shall any State deprive any person of life, liberty, or property, without due process of law; nor deny to any person within its jurisdiction the equal protection of the laws." Section 5. "Congress shall have power to enforce, by appropriate legislation, the provisions of this article." The language in Section 1 changes from "citizen" to "person." While a citizen requires birth, a person lacks proper definition, and by any reasonable measure should include babies in the womb from the moment of conception. It seems like the real battle is in the Congress.

The 3.1.10 Initiative

At the present time, there are 2 House Bills (H.R. 586; 681) and a Senate Bill (S.231) which clarify that under the 14th Amendment, the definition of "person" in Section 1 thereof includes all human life from the moment of conception. These Bills are currently in committee. Their numbers will change with the swearing in of each new session of Congress. Please contact your **3** Congressmen at least **1** time per month, urging them to introduce and/or pass these Bills into law. Please pass this on to at least **10** others. The giant of the status quo looms large but let us take up the cause - it may just go viral and, by the grace of God, accomplish more than we could ever imagine. Become an active participant in the 3.1.10 Initiative! Be…

Devoted to Life